DYNAMIC TRUTHS
for the
SPIRIT-FILLED LIFE

DYNAMIC TRUTHS
for the
SPIRIT-FILLED LIFE

by

C. S. LOVETT, M.A., B.D., D.D.

Director of Personal Christianity

author of

PERSONAL NEW TESTAMENT COMMENTARY
DEALING WITH THE DEVIL
WITNESSING MADE EASY
THE 100% CHRISTIAN

cover design by AL JAMISON

illustrated by LINDA LOVETT

Published by

PERSONAL CHRISTIANITY

Baldwin Park, California

This book is affectionately dedicated to

THE HOLY SPIRIT

For it is He who has revealed these things to us and it is He who certifies them to our hearts.

PRINTED IN THE UNITED STATES OF AMERICA

CONTENTS

Foreword 7

Chapter One— God's Program —"Earth" 11

Chapter Two— The Facts of Life 30
A study of man's different kinds of life gives the
student the true significance of spiritual life and death.
The fact that man is an eternal soul gives spiritual
life and death a surprising meaning.

Chapter Three— Christ Coming in the Spirit 46
The literal receiving of Christ in the Spirit is carefully
pictured in this study which deals with the actual
mechanics of salvation.

Chapter Four— The Depravity of Man 63
The fall of Adam and its effect upon the human race
produces a bondage from which only God's interven-
ing power can bring man's release.

Chapter Five— The Two Natures of the Believer 83
The receipt of a new nature offers the Christian deliverance from depravity. His struggle between the
two natures is pictured as the proper environment
for Christian maturity.

Chapter Six— Key Doctrines Explained
by the Two Natures 106
The believer's sin problem becomes simplified when
viewed from an understanding of the two natures:
Eternal security; Salvation and Rewards become crystal
clear.

Chapter Seven— Christ the First Christian 124
The believer discovers the secret of Christ's victory
over sin and learns how this victory has application
in His own personal experience.

Chapter Eight— The Sonship of the Believer 145
God's literal system for reproducing sons is viewed
with respect to the future adoption.

Chapter Nine— Victory Through the Indwelling Christ . 162

Here the secret of victory in the Christian life is discovered as practicing the presence of Christ. Some
practical suggestions are offered.

Chapter Ten— The Finality of the Christian Life 184

The relationship between the life on earth and the
life of heaven supplies urgency in living for Christ
now. Man's time is seen as his most valuable possession when he realizes he has but this one lifetime
to mature in Christ.

Some Questions? --- 205

FOREWORD

"I'M SAVED—now I can relax!"

Ever get that notion? Well you can forget it. You may have heard that all a person has to do is come to Jesus and all of his problems disappear. If you believe that, get ready for a shock. It just isn't true. Instead of bliss and ease following your decision for Christ, you have walked into a WAR!

Christianity is not for sissies. It's for fighters. You might as well know right now you've got a fight on your hands. Maybe I didn't need to say that. Perhaps you've already discovered how true it is. I wouldn't doubt it. The moment a Christian sets his heart on pleasing God, he finds he can't do it. A powerful drive inside him makes him WANT to do something else.

When he tries to pray, it doesn't come easily. His mind wanders. All sorts of scenes surface as he attempts to concentrate on the Lord. He'd like to study the Bible, but there's the compulsion to do other things. It seems that no matter what he wants to do for the Lord, his old life keeps tugging at him, prodding him to do something else. The pull is so powerful he often ends up doing things that displease the Lord.

Well that's the war. The awful part is you find yourself sinning—lots of times. You hate it, but you can't seem to help it. This situation has baffled more than one sincere Christian. The questions come: how can a true believer, one indwelt by the Holy Spirit, continually do those things which hurt the Lord even when he doesn't want to? What is this power of the old life that keeps us from doing what we should and makes us do that which we shouldn't?

You're about to learn the answer.

Every Christian has TWO natures. Until he is saved, he only has one. There was no struggle then, he simply did what he wanted. But once he was saved, he had another nature which was at war with his old one. Why? The old nature loves the old life and is headed for hell. The new nature loves the new life and is headed for heaven. This is why things never go easily for the Christian. His life is a series of trials and tribulations, failures and frustrations.

The old life is more powerful than the new one UNTIL the Christian learns HOW to develop strength in Christ. That's the purpose of this book. It explains God's wonderful program for bringing believers to maturity. It provides them with the insights necessary to understand the war and win it. A person cannot live the Spirit-filled life without winning this war. He can't begin to fight until he knows how. Everything you need to fathom the warfare of the Christian life is right here.

The teaching approach of this book is different. The truths are not only set forth in text form, but visually as well. Also there is a summary at the end of each lesson which serves to crystallize the main truths. These should be fixed in the reader's mind before he moves on to the next lesson.

Originally these insights were presented in two books which we called a follow-up program. The first teaching was set forth in "Follow-Up Made Easy," while the remaining nine lessons were called "Soul-Building Made Easy." The Holy Spirit did not want us to limit this material to new Christians only. Therefore, we have rearranged the truths to make them available to ALL Christians. We now have two books replacing the former ones.

The book you are now reading contains the basic truths needed for the Spirit-filled life. It presents all of the material once covered by our follow-up course. In addition, we have a TEACHER'S BOOK which shows how to communicate these truths either to a class or at the personal level. It's called "Teach Dynamic Truths." When you teach a class, the book you are now reading, "Dynamic Truths for the Spirit-Filled Life," becomes the students' text.

As you go through this book the first time, be sure to have your Bible handy. You will want to check the references shown on the charts and mentioned in the text. These will be KEY verses. Fix them in your mind. They not only make for solid understanding of the truths, but they become great ammunition when Satan presses an attack against the lesson. You can expect him to do it, so be ready for him.

After you finish each chapter, refer to the visual diagram. You'll find it, along with a main truth outline, at the end of the chapter. Go over both of them before you move on to the next lesson. This is a very effective learning method. Don't cheat yourself by skipping the charts, main truth outline, or the Bible references.

Now dear reader, get ready for a treat. The Lord is going to bless you with some startling truths. I doubt if you've heard these things before. Don't let Satan use that to bother you. Look to the Holy Spirit. He is your teacher. Check for His witness as you study. Once you get a real grip on these truths, the mystery of our Christian warfare will be gone. Once the truths get a grip on you, you'll find yourself living the Spirit-filled life!

Wait and see.

C. S. Lovett

CHAPTER ONE

GOD'S PROGRAM—"EARTH"

"There must be more to life than this!"

Haven't you said that to yourself more than once in your life? Sure, who hasn't? Who doesn't think about the endless routine of three meals a day, on the job, and back to bed? And for what? A grave? It doesn't make sense. Yet, as you watch people plodding aimlessly through years of that monotonous routine, heading straight for that grave, you hear very few asking about the meaning of life on earth.

It's almost as if no one wants to talk about it. And yet you know the haunting questions are there, "Who am I? Why am I here?" Those are perhaps the most important things anyone can face, yet people seem afraid to ask them. Is it because they fear there is no answer? Or is it because they don't want to look into the Bible? That is the only place you see, where such questions are answered. Only in God's Word is the mystery of life explained.

Once we turn to the precious Book, we find more than answers to those questions. We also find that life on earth is a tremendous adventure. It may not look like it to the person blindly trudging the squirrel cage of three meals a day. But to the one who sees life from God's vantage point, it is another story altogether. When we understand the amazing program God is carrying out in men on the earth, and behold our part in it, life is transformed from a boring routine to a fantastic adventure.

This world is no accident. Neither is our presence in it. It is part of a grand scheme that makes man the center of all events and reveals him as the apple of the Creator's eye. This volume, the Bible, which is before us is actually a black and white "blue print" of God's thrilling program in which are unraveled the mysteries of life. The promise to anyone who will "seek", is that he shall "find."

GOD'S PURPOSE IN MAN

The **fact** of God is questioned by very few. Somehow, there is a "built-in" witness to every heart that God **is.** Every civilized child, at least those growing up in this country, have some ideas concerning Him — ideas that include the fact that He is eternal and almighty. What child has not asked, "Where did God come from?", only to be told, "He always was." The slightest reasoning admits that this must be so for if God Himself were made, then the one who made Him would have to be God. No, only God can be God and He must be eternal. Man has been aware of this truth for all of recorded time and the testimony of God can be found among all peoples.

The first chapter of the first book of the Bible reveals man's beginning. What astonishing things are said: "Let us make man in our image and after our likeness." Man is at once revealed as resembling — yea, even a reproduction — of the Almighty God, Himself. What a testimony to the dignity of man, and what great expectations God must have had when those words were first uttered.

At a point in eternity, we don't know where, God made man and put him upon the earth. The account reveals that the earth was made first, and then man placed upon it. Probably the first question to enter minds here is, "Why did God make man?" Granted that man is made in the image of God, why is he made at all? Why does God bother with a physical creation, and then put man on it?

12

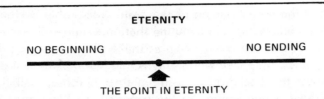

ETERNITY

NO BEGINNING   NO ENDING

THE POINT IN ETERNITY

Eternity has no beginning or ending. At some point in eternity God said, "Let us make man." When this took place, we do not know, for it occurred outside of space and time. We do not have any tools for examining eternity. Logic and reason are not able to go beyond the three dimensions of space or fathom the compression of time. Yet it appears that the entire human story from Genesis to Revelation is somehow compressed into that ONE DOT on the line above.

The obvious answer is: for Himself. Many passages clue us as to why God did all this. John, writing under the inspiration of the Holy Spirit, lays stress on the fact that God's reason for man and the earth is **fellowship.** God made man that He might have fellowship with him. Of course, this is why man is made in the image of God. The God and man fellowship would have to be one where each is capable of enjoying the other. The Revelation, the last book of the Bible, ends on this note of fellowship. It tells us when time has ceased to be, God will be in the midst of His people enjoying them as a Father with His children. (Rev. 21:3-7).

The Father and son relationship is often repeated throughout the Bible. Before one finally closes the cover on the Sacred Testimony he is convinced that this is the grand goal of the human experiment.

It is this future fellowship that supplies the **key** to understanding God's dealing with men. If the fellowship is to be genuine and have meaning, it follows that man must be capable of entering into such a relationship. Man must be able to take part or share or make some contribution for this is the very meaning of the term, "fellowship." That's what a fellowship is — a mutual sharing, acting and reacting with others. For such a thing to take place, man must be possessed of a free will. The whole story of man is set against this backdrop of God's eternal purpose. All that is found within history, or the pages of the Bible must be consistent with His eternal goal of the glorious fellowship.

When Genesis declares man to be made in the image of God, the least that it can mean is that man is representative of God. Many have sought to give the phrase various meanings, but reduced to the barest minimum it holds that man is like God. Regardless of any treatment the passage must suffer, the declaration is simple. Man is the **image of God.** This truth demands that certain things be so with respect to man.

There are some things, which if they are true concerning God, must also be true of man. Surely, there is one point where man must resemble God. That is in his ability to choose and determine his own destiny. If man is not free at this point, how can he be said to be the image of God? This is so obviously true concerning the object, it cannot be missing in the image. If this is lacking, man is not a reflection, or image, of God at all.

When the Commandments demand that the creature love the Creator in such terms as, "thou shalt love the Lord thy God with all thy heart . . . ," it is immediately manifest that here is something which cannot be done unless the creature is **free** to do so. If man is not free to obey or disobey God, the giving of any laws would be pointless.

Another feature in which man must resemble God is in His spiritual being. If God is a spirit being, an unquestioned claim, then the image must be also. To this any psychologist would agree. Modern psychology is the study of **unseen** man. Man is really a **spiritual** being. It's true that he has a body, but he, himself, is not a body. One look at any body, before it is lowered into a grave, is sufficient proof of this. The body frame is still intact, yet the person is obviously gone.

No, man is not a body. He has a body. It merely serves to reveal the person that lives inside. Even the brain can be found undisturbed within a corpse. Hence it, too, is but a tool of the spirit-man who once dwelt within the temporal house. This is why psychologists distinguish between the mind and the brain. They are not the same. One belongs to the spirit-man, and the other to his body. One is the tool of the other.

Man, himself, is spirit. And like God, whom he resembles, is invisible. What is seen of him, however, is the personality that is manifested through the physical organism of the body. Thus we find that not only the earth, but man's body as well, is a part of the physical creation that was instituted to receive man for the temporary human experiment.

THE FIRST SIX DAYS OF CREATION

GOD'S PURPOSE IN THE EARTH

That for which God longs is man's **freely offered** love. God, since He is a God of love, needs love, and someone to love. This is His motive for making man in the first place. Man alone is made in His image. Man alone, of all beings, is capable of returning His love. Not only does the first commandment, but also the cross reveal the desperate hunger that God has for the love of man. His great passion can be satisfied only by man's freely offered love.

The fact of man's freedom to obey or not obey is one that raises problems for God. Man, since he is free to decide for himself, may or may not elect to love God. He may prefer to love another object, or even himself, rather than God. Inasmuch as the eternal fellowship can only include those who love God, it must first be determined **who** or **what** man will love. Only those who voluntarily decide to unite with God in fellowship will be included in that eternal circle. Therefore, God devised an ingenious test — a test calculated to determine just where each man, employing his own free will, would elect to place his love and devotion. This test is the whole program "EARTH" — the entire story of man in the world for all of time.

A test, it is to be noted, has a beginning and an ending. This at once distinguishes it from eternity which has neither beginning nor ending. The "test" is a **temporary** device. It does not last forever. It is this feature that introduces us to the subject of **time.**

Time properly includes the whole story of man and the earth, together. Biblically it is represented by the period from Genesis through the events predicted in the Revelation, and all that which is included in the term "history." The whole of it is recorded in this wonderful Book which God has given us, our Bible. Here is the story of man on the earth and God's dealing with him in order to test his free will.

THE BIBLE ACCOUNT OF MAN'S TESTING

Looking at time in the Bible, we find that while God is testing man with respect to his will, the **method** of His dealing with him is not always the same. In fact, we can observe five distinct changes in His methods. Yet, even though we notice that the methods are different, the test is always the same. God really has but one test for man. Thus, for the purposes of our study we find it convenient to divide time into five unequal periods, yet we are careful not to break up our Bible into five sections. There is just one story of God and man. It is unfolded progressively throughout the entire Biblical narrative. Our five periods are treated as stages in the advancing revelation. Better yet, perhaps, our type of study is something like looking into a house through five separate windows. The scene is not always the same, but it is always the same house. When we add the scenes of the five windows we have the whole story of God's program as revealed in the Bible.

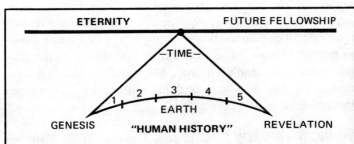

A folded picture SKETCH of the FIVE WINDOWS came with your book. It pictures God's different methods of dealing with man on the earth. Place it in front of you where you can refer to it easily as we discuss God's working in each of the windows. In the next few minutes you will behold the entire human panorama from Genesis to Revelation. You will be able to follow the drama as it unfolds, for the story flows along the RED LINE.

17

Now let's begin, taking each window in order. We'll view this marvellous parade of events, some of which are past, some future, and some which have to do with us right now.

WINDOW NUMBER ONE (History's Beginning)

The story of God and man begins for us in the garden of Eden. Here the first pair, Adam and Eve, are seen as the founders of the human race. They enjoy the presence of the Lord and have no burdensome responsibilities placed upon them other than caring for the garden and partaking of its blessings.

There was one restriction, however, they were not to eat of the fruit of one particular tree. Their desire to obey God and continue in fellowship with Him was put to the test at this point. Remember, we said that the earth provides a testing place for man. This was the test for the starters of the human race.

Their failure to obey God in this single test is responsible for the entrance of sin into the world. "Wherefore as by one man's disobedience sin entered into the world . . . " is the way that Paul puts it. The succeeding generations of all humanity have suffered the effect of their fateful decision. Bible history marks this tragic event as the fall of man. The story of the first testing in the garden ended in man's failure. As we close the first window, we see the man and his wife being driven from the presence of the Lord.

WINDOW NUMBER TWO (God's Dealing With Mankind Generally — The Nations)

With the fall of man in the garden, humanity acquired a "taste" for evil. All of Adam's heirs would be responsible to distinguish between right and wrong, for now this distinction was a matter of **conscience**. From Adam, man inherited the knowledge of good and evil. Now he was accountable for the use of that knowledge. Knowledge always brings responsibility. No longer was it a matter of a single choice of obedience, as it was for the first pair. Now the races that issued from Adam and Eve would have to judge for themselves whether things were right or not in the sight of God.

The "sin" story continues with the murder of Abel. Through our window we observe that the rise of all the nations emerges from this ugly and violent beginning. Man multiplies and soon the earth is filled with wicked and brutal men. So corrupt is man and so heedless of his own conscience that God appears to be on the verge of abandoning the whole human experiment.

Apparently there is but one righteous family in all the earth — that of Noah. These eight people are delivered out of the devastating flood by means of a specially prepared ark. Out of Noah's three sons God again peoples the earth. With the introduction of different languages these are scattered throughout the regions of the Near East and Europe. This view of God's dealing with mankind generally, ends with the nations failing to walk before God and serve Him. The races fail in the testing at the point of their own **consciences** and thus a new program or method of dealing was to come into operation.

WINDOW NUMBER THREE (God's Dealing Through One Nation — Israel)

This scene in which God deals with one nation, instead of mankind generally, has its beginning with the call of Abram out of Ur of the Chaldees. Here again, as in the case of Noah, there was but one family out of the earth's people that truly worshipped God. This one man was led by God out of his heathen nation into what was later called the land of Israel. God chose the man, and He also chose the land. With these He was to build for Himself a nation that would represent Him and His message to the world. When Abram's faithfulness was truly determined, his name was changed to Abraham.

God promised this one man that He would make a nation from his heir. He kept that promise repeating it to Isaac, Abraham's son, and again to Jacob, his grandson. Out of Jacob, whose name God also changed to Israel, came twelve sons. These came to be known historically as the leaders of the twelve tribes of Israel.

It took time for this little family to grow into a nation. About four hundred years of that time were spent down in the land of Egypt where the Israelites were disciplined and schooled as the slaves of the foreign empire. Some of the Israeli-Egyptian bitterness today is traceable to that time when the people of God were being readied for nation-hood and their journey back to the land.

When the time arrived for their commissioning as a nation, God raised up a man from their midst who was to be their leader. It was Moses, whose task it was to lead the Israelites across the Red Sea and to gather them before God at Mount Sinai. In a solemn moment God spoke to the whole nation and delivered into their hands the code of law and life known as the Ten Commandments.

God entered into a covenant with them. They were commissioned from that day forth to be His personal and chosen nation to represent Him among all nations of the earth. They were to carry His appeal to all men and live a life that vindicated His message. They, themselves, were to reflect His holiness. It took forty years of wilderness wandering before the little nation was sufficiently disci-plined in matters of faith to the point where Joshua could lead them into the Promised Land.

The history of Israel, the select nation of God, in the land that was promised to Abraham, is also one of failure. Not only did Israel fail to be a clear light of revelation to the rest of the world, but she became contaminated with the false religions about her and frequently forsook the worship of God, who had called her into existence.

The nation grew and prospered under the kingship of Saul, David, and Solomon, but survived only as God divinely protected His people. Within three hundred years the empire was split and the northern part was taken into captivity by a powerful and savage nation. The southern part endured but one hundred and fifty years longer and then her idolatry and disobedience took her into the captivity of Babylon. This seventy-year disciplinary action was brought to pass by God to teach the new and small nation that her existence depended upon Him. It was effective teaching too, for never again was the nation to become guilty of openly worshipping other gods.

The nation of Israel was through as a witness to the world about her. She still has a ministry before her yet today, but her unique role as a nation scattering the darkness of heathendom was ended. A small group returned from the land of captivity to reoccupy the land of Palestine, but never again did she rise to become a significant power. Until this century she never regained control of Palestine, but continued to exist only as the vassal of other powers. This too had a singular purpose.

Through the remnant of the former nation was to come the One who would deliver mankind from the ruin and chaos that followed the tragedy of Eden. Out of this pitiful handful of Israelites was to come the Saviour of the world — the Messiah of Israel. The once proud nation remained huddled as a pathetic mandate of the Roman empire, dreaming of the day when the Saviour-King would arrive to restore the former glory. This was their great hope. Unfortunately they were so blinded by the fanatical desire to be restored to power, that they missed the Saviour when finally He did enter the human scene.

21

One of Israel's last acts of rebellion was to crucify her own Saviour and King, the Lord Jesus Christ. Her desire for world prominence and prestige caused her to refuse a carpenter's son as the promised Messiah. Blinded by passion and sin, the nation that was closest to God could not recognize Him, whose coming had been foretold in their own sacred writings. The end came quickly, for the once highly-favored nation lasted but seventy years after the birth of Jesus. She disappeared among the nations of the world with the destruction of the city of Jerusalem in A.D. 70.

WINDOW NUMBER FOUR (God's Dealing Through Individuals — The Church)

With the commissioning of the disciples and the ascension of the Lord into heaven, the method of God's dealing with man changed once again. The message, of· course, is the very same one that has been sounded from the beginning — love God and obey Him. Now God's appeal comes from individuals rather than a nation.

For two thousand years individual Christians have felt their personal responsibility to carry the revelation of God into their own particular world. Right where they are they live for Christ and tell of His love and concern for all men. During His earthly ministry Christ was referred to as **The** Light of the World. Now, in His visible absence from the earth, these Christians serve as "many lights." Men in Europe, Asia, Africa, and the Western continents live individually unto God so that over the whole world there is sprinkled the Word of divine revelation.

Even today, it is clear that mankind is in no mood to turn to God. Perhaps, in greater numbers than ever before, certain ones are turning to Him seeking forgiveness, but the nations are as unconcerned as ever. Thus the Bible predicts the failure of this present method. The scene through our fourth window, even though it is not yet concluded, is hastening toward failure.

Man just will not turn to God even when the "way" is provided and sounded with unmistakable clearness. The message goes out over all the earth, "whosoever **will** may come." God appeals always to man's will. "Come," he says, "and partake of the gift of Eternal Life." All that is required is the turning of the heart unto the Lord and allowing Him, with His power, to redirect the life. But men, generally, will have none of it — thus only judgment can await.

The Bible foresees the time, probably not too far distant now, when the church will be literally removed from the earth. Then its ministry of proclaiming God's loving appeal will have ceased. Man will be permitted to run the course of his ungodly rebellion. He will be able to sin without restraint and it will take him into the holocaust described as the "battle of Armageddon".

Man, in his unleashed degredation, will be allowed to spend his fury upon man. The Scripture observes, that because of the devastation, "except those days be shortened, there should no flesh be saved . . . " (Matt. 24:22). The days will be shortened when God intervenes at the return of Christ in triumphant glory to bring the carnage to an end. Our fourth window pictures for us man still refusing to walk in fellowship with his Creator and the catastrophe that this invariably brings.

WINDOW NUMBER FIVE (The Personal Reign of Christ on Earth)

A fifth method of God's dealing with man has yet to be instituted and its occasion will be the personal and visible return of Jesus Christ to the earth — this time not as the humble carpenter of Nazareth, but as the Lord of Heaven. Now He comes as one might well expect Him to, in a dazzling, spectacular blaze of glory that fills all the earth with His presence.

Our scene now is one much like the grand finale of a staged drama. Assembled will be all of the nations that survive the terrible battle of Armageddon. Present also will be the regathered nation of Israel. There are yet unfulfilled promises made to the patriarch Abraham that must be accomplished in this people in order that the Word of God might remain steadfast. The Church will be there too, to share in Christ's reign of glory.

Whereas in the past stages of man's history, God dealt first with the nations, then one particular nation, and finally through the individuals of the Church, now all three agencies are arrayed in a simultaneous pageantry. What a grand finale!

We see also the world ruled by a "rod of iron." Peace, blessing, and prosperity come to man and all the earth is filled with the knowledge of the Lord. In this last method, God uses force. He sees to it that the earth is at rest. By means of His power, the programs which formerly were failures, now are crowned with success. He deals with the nations and is successful. He employs the nation of Israel once again and here, too, is successful. The church also fulfills its glorious ministry.

Everywhere, and in all three forms of dealing, God is vindicated and glorified. Even the land gives forth her fruit so that every place there is nothing but evidence of God's abundant goodness and blessing. No wonder the world is filled with the knowledge of the Lord as Zechariah claims! The nations proclaim Him! Israel proclaims Him! You and I will proclaim Him! All together, in a great chorus singing and shouting Hosannas that rock the very portals of Heaven. It is no wonder that "from the highest to the lowest," they shall all know Him.

But alas, how all this is to prove the desperate character of man. He is determined to walk contrary to God in spite of everything that has been revealed. The loosing of Satan, who has been bound for the thousand golden years, finds man's heart still prefering the "tempter's" offer to God's loving plea. The Kingdom of Christ on earth, which serves as the **final test** of man's will, reveals that mankind generally, cares nothing for God. In spite of the combined witness of the nations, the people Israel, and the Church — in spite of the "garden of Eden" setting with the Lord's personal ministrations — man finally reveals that there is nothing God can do to him to make him change his mind.

Once man has tasted of sin, the fact stands that he prefers it to anything God can offer him. This is true of mankind generally, though we have seen that some do, by His Grace, elect to love Him. Praise God, we are among that number. There is nothing left now but to conclude the human story and bring the experiment to an end.

Thus it is that the program "Earth" serves as an ingenious separating device. Man has, by the exercise of his own free will, determined his own destiny. God allows the choice to stand. Those who freely turn to God, may be judged as having **passed the test** and are thus qualified to spend eternity with Him. Those who, during the space of their lifetime, reject His plea are doomed to an eternity separated from Him.

Man is created an eternal soul and he will spend eternity someplace. **Where** he spends it is up to him. He has just the single probationary span of his life on the earth to decide, and **his decision is his own.** Man is given this one opportunity and that's all—" . . . it is appointed unto men once to die, and after that, the judgment" (Heb. 9:27).

CONCLUSION

Thus we have seen the whole story of man as outlined in the Bible. Our windows have been useful, but what a tragic sight they have pictured. Man's failure abounds everywhere. And yet, in the midst of all the gloom, there shines the glory of God. No doubt, you who read this book are saved and can look forward with joy to the eternal fellowship. What's important now, is **preparing** for that "face to face" fellowship with Jesus. The chief significance of this life is the opportunity it affords to prepare for that day.

HERE'S WHAT WE HAVE LEARNED SO FAR:

1. The world in which we live is no accident. It is the center of a carefully worked out plan.

2. The earth, along with human history, is a temporary testing device for man's free will.

3. We have seen how we are involved in God's plan and where we fit into the whole of Bible history.

4. We have discovered the relationship of time to eternity. It shows us that we ought to invest ourselves in Christ rather than the passing things of this world.

5. Now that we understand God's plan, life on earth makes sense. We can adjust ourselves to the divine program and have a satisfying basis for living unto the next life rather than this one.

6. We also know what God means when He says, "Lay up for yourselves treasure in heaven." Why should a man invest his time and money in the things of this life when he is going to spend eternity with God? The wisest investment a man can make is to pour his one life into Christ.

GOD'S PROGRAM—"EARTH"

MAIN TEACHING (Review and Remember)

1. God exists eternally.

2. God made man in His own image so that He could enjoy him in fellowship.

3. The planned fellowship is eternal; therefore, man must be eternal also.

4. For man to be in the image of God he must be self-determining as well as possess a free will.

5. Since man is possessed of a free will, a test is necessary to determine what he will do with this freedom.

6. The test that God devised may be called the human experiment or history.

7. A test, however, has a beginning and an ending. This test or human history is called "Time."

8. Time may be viewed as God's dealing with man through five distinct movements. We have labeled these movements, "windows," and through them observe the one story of God and man.

9. Each man is given opportunity to respond to God's program—some accept and some reject.

10. Man determines his own destiny by free choice. Believers anticipate the eternal fellowship; rejectors condemn themselves to eternal hell.

11. When the earth, a giant whirling separator, has served its purpose, it passes away and time is concluded.

12. Fellowship with God is seen to be more vital than anything the earth can offer: one simply serves the other.

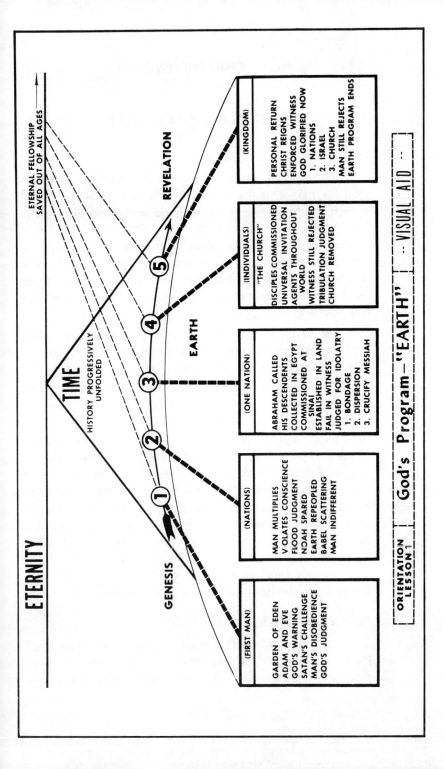

ETERNITY

ETERNAL FELLOWSHIP
SAVED OUT OF ALL AGES

TIME

HISTORY PROGRESSIVELY
UNFOLDED

GENESIS

REVELATION

EARTH

(FIRST MAN)

GARDEN OF EDEN
ADAM AND EVE
GOD'S WARNING
SATAN'S CHALLENGE
MAN'S DISOBEDIENCE
GOD'S JUDGMENT

(NATIONS)

MAN MULTIPLIES
VIOLATES CONSCIENCE
FLOOD JUDGMENT
NOAH SPARED
EARTH REPEOPLED
BABEL SCATTERING
MAN INDIFFERENT

(ONE NATION)

ABRAHAM CALLED
HIS DESCENDENTS
COLLECTED IN EGYPT
COMMISSIONED AT
SINAI
ESTABLISHED IN LAND
FAIL IN WITNESS
JUDGED FOR IDOLATRY
1. BONDAGE
2. DISPERSION
3. CRUCIFY MESSIAH

(INDIVIDUALS)

"THE CHURCH"

DISCIPLES COMMISSIONED
UNIVERSAL INVITATION
AGENTS THROUGHOUT
WORLD
WITNESS STILL REJECTED
TRIBULATION JUDGMENT
CHURCH REMOVED

(KINGDOM)

PERSONAL RETURN
CHRIST REIGNS
ENFORCED WITNESS
GOD GLORIFIED NOW
1. NATIONS
2. ISRAEL
3. CHURCH
MAN STILL REJECTS
EARTH PROGRAM ENDS

ORIENTATION
LESSON 1 — God's Program—"EARTH" — VISUAL AID --

CHAPTER TWO

THE FACTS OF LIFE

Review

In our first chapter we saw the overall program of God for man and the earth. We noticed particularly that man is made in the image of God and designed, in his being, to spend eternity with God. Thus man is properly created for eternity rather than for the brief span of earthly life alone — created for eternal fellowship with God. For this fellowship man needs to have a free will, since there can be no fellowship unless all parties are able to enter into free exchange.

The earth, we learned, is a temporary program that God ingeniously employs as a testing device for man's freedom of choice. Man's will needs to be tested to see what he will do with it before the final, eternal state can be entered.

During the course of man's earthly probation, which today approaches three score and ten years, God reveals Himself to each man. He has been making this revelation progressively to all men down through the course of history. Within the span of each man's life there comes to him some revealed knowledge of God upon which he must act in his own free choice. It is man's response to this revelation that determines his future status. While some elect, as we know, to learn more of God and obey Him, others spurn Him. It is man's choice, at this point, that determines whether he spends eternity in heaven or in hell.

MAN'S DIFFERENT KINDS OF LIFE

How many kinds of life do you suppose Adam had? He had three and they all have names which you have probably heard before. He had **physical** life, **psychological** life, and **spiritual** life. We can find all three of these kinds of life in the second chapter of Genesis.

Let's look now at the verse that perhaps tells us the most about man's formation: Genesis 2:7. Here we read, "And the Lord God formed man out of the dust of the ground and breathed into his nostrils the **BREATH OF LIFE** . . ." Let's look first at just that much.

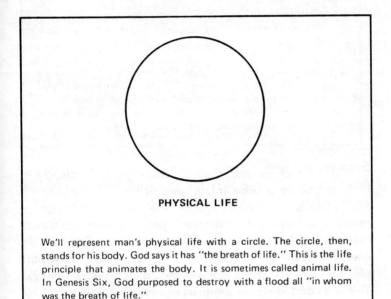

PHYSICAL LIFE

We'll represent man's physical life with a circle. The circle, then, stands for his body. God says it has "the breath of life." This is the life principle that animates the body. It is sometimes called animal life. In Genesis Six, God purposed to destroy with a flood all "in whom was the breath of life."

Now recall an important observation. Man is not a body. He **has** a body. The man, himself, dwells within this **living** body. Man is a **soul,** not a body. But what about that soul? It is a **living** soul. We discover this when we read further, " . . . and man became a LIVING soul." Not only does a man's body have life, but so does a man's soul. It lives too. Thus we find there is **body** life, and there is **soul** life.

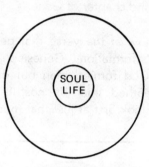

PHYSICAL LIFE

The Greek word for soul is **psuche** from which comes our modern word "psychology" and refers to the unseen part of man. Tests conducted by psychologists measure a number of human factors which function independently of the body. By means of these tests, the clinicians construct a profile of the person living inside the body.

The life of the soul we call "soul-life," scientifically it is described as **psuche-life** or **psychic-life.** The energy of this soul-life or psychic-life is that which activates a man's personality. Even as physical life animates man's muscles and body functions, so is soul-life used for thinking and feeling processes. The operation of the soul is carried out by means of psychic energy. This is a completely different work from that performed by the body. No one can see a man thinking or watch his feelings. They are invisible processes, yet they are real.

The work of the soul or person is carried on as a separate functioning so that the soul can exist apart from the body. In fact the soul has to do this when the body dies. All physical death really means is that the body can no longer be used by the man who lives inside. The living man needs a **living** body which can respond to his orders. When death comes to the body, the person who lives inside must depart.

The truth of man's immortality gives theology, (the study of divine things) a distinct advantage over secular psychological theory. Christian psychology does not agree with those moderns who hold that **psychic** energy comes from transformed vital energy of one's **body.** Consider what it would mean if this were so. It would mean that the soul dies when the body dies. Certainly this is not the Christian point of view. Christianity insists on the immortality of man, asserting that all men live somewhere after death. Why, even sinners are declared to **live eternally** in hell.

Here is a truth that brings us to another weighty observation. What kind of life do sinners have in hell? If we grant, and we do, that they live there eternally, what kind of a life do they possess? It can't be physical life, that's gone. Their bodies are in the grave. They wouldn't be in hell if they still had physical life.

Could it be that they have spiritual life? No, certainly not the spiritual life of which the New Testament speaks. That gift has been refused. They are there in the first place because they have refused the **gift of life** that God offers. No, it can only be a **third** form of life — one which grants them this LIVING death in hell. It has to be the life which we've discussed — psychic-life.

A further thing to note is, since **all** men are made for eternity, **all** men are equipped with eternal, psychic-life. It is certainly the divine intention that all men should spend eternity with God. It is true that not all will — yet God appeals to all to come unto Him showing no respect or partiality toward any. Not only are all men made in His image, but all are equipped with **His own** psychic-life. The future fellowship is one where **eternal** beings enjoy one another. No man is created just to come into this world and die here. That view certainly is not Christian. No man is created just for the earth experience, but for eternity.

Every man therefore has eternal, psychic-life, and this is the way that he comes into the world. He is born an eternal, immortal soul and is made for eternity. An important difference is now discovered; the difference between men in heaven or hell is not in the peculiar kind of psychic-life they possess, but WHERE they spend it. The distinction between those in heaven and hell, as we find it in this lesson, is where they live out the **same** psychic-life.

One **lives** in hell and the other **lives** in heaven, but both possess the same kind of psychic-life. They are both living souls created for the eternal state. Separated from their bodies they live in different places. This very thought raises another important question.

WHAT THEN IS THE SPIRITUAL LIFE OF WHICH THE BIBLE SPEAKS?

If all men have the same kind of psychic-life and there is no difference in the life between those in heaven or hell — just what is the spiritual death and life of which the New Testament speaks? The Word clearly refers to those who are spiritually alive and those who are spiritually dead. What is meant by these terms?

The answer to this question is also found in our second chapter of Genesis, verse seventeen. Here is God's warning to Adam, "In the **day** that thou eatest thereof thou shalt surely **die**." Remembering that God instructed Adam that he was not to partake of the "tree of the knowledge of good and evil," He now is promising **death** to Adam if he disobeys. This is a death that has to do with sin and disobedience. What kind of a death is it?

First, we ask ourselves, was it a physical death? Did Adam die physically that day? Certainly not. He lived nearly 930 years beyond that day. Was it psychic-life that was taken away from him? Was it psychic-death that he died? No, it couldn't be that either, for to lose the life of the soul would mean that he would pass out of existence.

It would mean that he was anihilated and we know that was not so. Since it is not physical death that is referred to here and since it is not psychic-death, then obviously it has to be another kind.

Now, what did happen to Adam that day? Actually he was driven from the presence of the Lord. He was driven out of the garden so that the fellowship between him and God was broken. This is what happened to Adam that day. Thus the death that is referred to, is the **separation** of Adam from God. The line between Adam (the living soul) and God was now broken and he is said to have died. This is the real death as far as God is concerned. It is God's great heartache. Thus it receives His special emphasis in the Word. What the Bible really means when it speaks of spiritual death is the separated state of living souls from God.

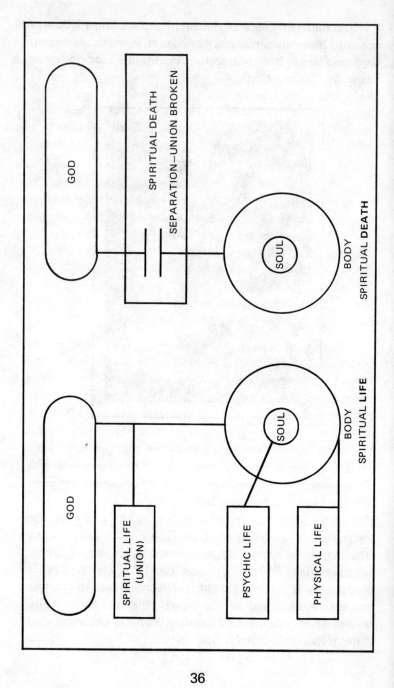

36

A man may possess physical life; that is, his body functions so that he walks about the earth breathing and performing all the things peculiar to physical existence. He may also have psychic-life; that is, he personally thinks, feels, and gives vent to passion as well as doing all of the things relative to soul-life. He is regarded as **spiritually dead,** however, unless he is joined to God. Unless he is joined to God, he is dead as far as the Bible is concerned, even though physically alive.

This becomes clear when we examine Paul's words to the spiritually-alive Ephesians, "you who were **DEAD** in trespasses and sins . . . " he says to them, referring to their former separated state. They had physical life and psychic-life and yet they were regarded as dead. Certainly their state of death did not mean that they were physically dead. Nor could it have meant that they ceased to have psychic-life. These Ephesians had both in their former state. They did not have fellowship or union with God.

Paul's use of the term death has to do with the SEPARATION OF LIVING BEINGS from God. This is the unique part of our lesson. We are accustomed to thinking of death as the taking away of the life substance from a person, but this is not so in the case of spiritual death. The death here has nothing to do with the soul itself; that is, no change occurs within the soul any more than a change takes place within a person's being when he is married or divorced. It is simply a state of union or separation that occurs.

Since man is created for God he is regarded as LOST unless he is united with God. This is where the expressions "lost" and "saved" come from. A man is lost until he is joined to God. Actually however, he is only lost to God. He is not lost to himself. He is not lost as far as he is concerned. He knows what he wants and is willing to spend a lifetime getting it. He doesn't think he is lost at all. Yet he is — to God. God made man for Himself, and when they are separated from each other, He is denied the use and pleasure which man can give him. Spiritual death then, we repeat, is a state of **disunion** between man and God.

What is spiritual life then? Spiritual life is just the **opposite** of spiritual death. If spiritual death is the separation of God and man, spiritual life is the **UNION** of God and man. The two ideas are uniquely combined in a popular verse — one which is used by almost every soul-winner — "For the wages of sin is death, but the gift of God is eternal life . . . " (Rom. 6:23). Here the wages of sin, or spiritual death, refers to the human-divine **separation**. The gift of life has to do with the **reunion**. It is in this sense that Jesus is "the Life," for it is He Who restores man to God. The union is accomplished by Him. Hence He can say, "I am the . . . Life . . . " (John 14:6).

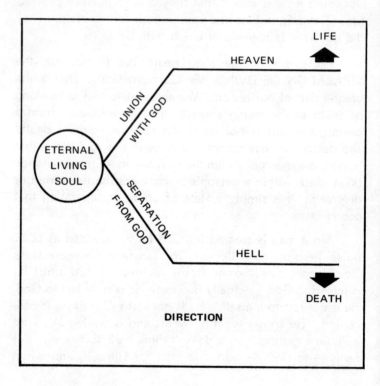

A most important thing to notice is that neither spiritual life nor death has anything to do with the psychological life of the soul. It remains intact with nothing added or taken away. In neither death nor life, as referred to here, does any change take place within the soul itself. The big difference between the lost and saved is one of **DIRECTION** — where each is going. Both are going to spend eternity some place. The man who has spiritual life is headed for heaven, while the man who is classed as spiritually dead, is headed for hell. Both have the very same soul-life, but they will live it in entirely different places. Now we have one more important question to ask ourselves.

HOW DOES UNION WITH GOD COME TO MAN?

If a man is separated from God, how can he be united with Him? God's vast love for man is instantly revealed the moment this question is considered. How desperately He must love man! A person might think that God would wipe out the whole of creation when Adam sinned and man fell — but He didn't. Why didn't He start over again with a new race of people once mankind was lost to Him through Adam's transgression?

The answer lies in the fact that man was made for a unique purpose. The important truth and one which is not often thought through, is that man was made FOR GOD TO LOVE. Man was not made just to love God. That's the emphasis that we usually hear, that the first duty of the creature is to love the Creator. True it is, but that isn't the only reason man was created. God is a God of love, and a God of love **needs someone** to love. There's no point in being a lover unless there is someone for Him to love. He is the Great Lover. He was "head over heels" in love with man from the very beginning of the human experiment.

39

So God, because of His great love for man, instead of destroying His creation planned to redeem it. He couldn't abandon man. He was, in a most reverent sense, "over a barrel" because of His desperate passion for His loved ones. He was willing and even today is still willing to do everything to restore the creation to Himself. It is this love that takes us to the depths of John 3:16 where we find that, "God so **LOVED** the **World** that He gave His only begotten Son . . ." The cross forever stands as a measure of God's consumate passion for man and His determination to save him for Himself. There is no other explanation for this supreme act; no other explanation for the salvation of man through Christ, other than this consuming dedication to His creation. Only in the light of this love does the cross make sense.

In order for God to save man, more was required than His simple offer of forgiveness. The redemption goes far beyond the idea of forgiving man. Forgiveness alone could not begin to accomplish the reconciliation God sought. To us it appears that way. We hear God's invitation, "Come to Me and I'll forgive you" and we are tempted to think of salvation in terms of forgiveness alone. For God the matter was far more complicated than that.

Man's separation from God was due in the first place to the depraved nature he acquired as a result of being born in the line of Adam. The fall, back in the Garden of Eden, effected a change in Adam's nature — a change in Adam himself. As Adam's newly acquired depraved nature was passed on to his heirs, **all men** became the enemies of God by **nature**. Paul insists that this is the case when he again reminds the Ephesians of their former state, "And were by **nature**, the children of wrath, even as others." (Eph. 2:3)

God's problem in saving man is seen more clearly now. Man needs more than forgiveness — he needs to be changed. **Forgiving a person does not change his nature.** If a person steals, he remains a thief, regardless of whether he is forgiven or not. Dying for a person will not change him either. Even the death of God's Son upon the cross will not change men, any more than would paying for someone's theft mean that the culprit was no longer a thief. Regardless of anything that is done **for** us, we are still depraved beings and possess natures that make us enemies of God. It follows that God must deal with our natures if He is to reconcile us to Himself.

Further, we see that the problem squarely belongs to God. Man cannot change himself. As the leopard cannot change its own spots and the brain surgeon cannot operate on his own brain, neither can man change his own nature. It is something that God must do within man. If God is to bring men to Himself, then He must find a way to deal with man's nature.

Of course, this is why Jesus came to earth as God in human form. He came as He did, to do two important

41

things in behalf of man. One, to reveal to us just how much He loves man and how desperately He wants him. Second, to provide a new and righteous nature that will **equip** men for eternity with a Righteous God. The plight of sinners in heaven would be an impossible one, if by their very own natures they sought to live contrary to His desire. Certainly heaven is no place for man still in his depravity. Quite obviously, men cannot enter heaven without a change of nature.

If man is a sinner because of his nature, then it is because of that nature that man is separated from God. This is the point where God must center his redemptive program if man is to be made eligible for the eternal fellowship. He does, too. He does it by coming personally into each life where the door is opened to Him and making the needed changes.

Since the earthly program is one that appeals to man's free will, then clearly, the Lord's coming into lives is not a matter of force. He does not impose Himself upon anyone. To as many as will receive Him however, He is willing to come into their hearts and create a whole new nature that equips man for the heavenly state.

Since the Christ that comes into our hearts and lives is God, then we are, in the same moment, **united** with God in a literal union. If life means union, as we have seen it does, then this is how the gift of spiritual life comes to men.

In this study we have seen that man has three kinds of life. Physical, which permits the body to live by itself; psychic, which gives eternal liveliness to the soul; and spiritual life, which simply describes the state of the

42

soul — that is, its union with God. Also we've seen that spiritual life and death have nothing to do with the adding or taking away of life particles from the soul. Finally, we have learned spiritual life comes to man as he literally receives Christ — an experience which not only joins him to God, but equips and prepares him for the presence of the Lord in heaven.

Note: Those of the Arminian tradition, who teach a conditional salvation, will appreciate that the spiritual lifeline is connected by faith. Consistent with your approach to salvation, you could show that the line is attached to the individual only for so long as he continues to exercise faith in the Lord Jesus. Should he **destroy** his faith through worldliness or abandonment, then you could show the line as broken and his salvation forfeited. While my own view is that a union established by God cannot be broken by man, I must leave room for those whose views vary from mine.

THE FACTS OF LIFE

MAIN TEACHING (Review and Remember)

1. Adam had three kinds of life: (a) physical, (b) psychic, (c) spiritual.

2. The body has physical life which is temporal; the soul has psychic-life which is eternal.

3. All men have eternal, psychic-life, both in heaven and in hell, because they are designed to live forever.

4. The difference between those in heaven and those in hell is not in the kind of psychic-life they possess, but **where** they spend it.

5. Spiritual death is the separation of eternal, living souls from God.

6. Spiritual life is the union of eternal, living souls with God.

7. Spiritual death and spiritual life are **states** of the soul's existence rather than the granting or removing of any life substance. Illustration: marriage & divorce.

8. With either spiritual life or death, nothing happens within the soul itself—instead, a change of direction occurs.

9. When a man receives Christ, he is united with God. The Bible calls this union spiritual life or eternal life.

10. It is man's sinful nature that causes his separation from God. The coming of Christ into one's life effects a change in his nature as well as uniting him with God.

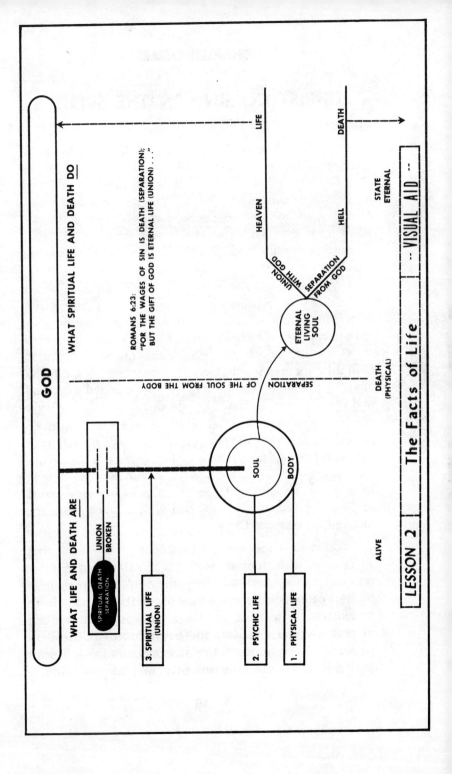

GOD

WHAT SPIRITUAL LIFE AND DEATH DO

ROMANS 6:23:
"FOR THE WAGES OF SIN IS DEATH (SEPARATION);
BUT THE GIFT OF GOD IS ETERNAL LIFE (UNION) . . ."

LIFE

DEATH

HEAVEN

HELL

STATE
ETERNAL

UNION WITH GOD

SEPARATION FROM GOD

ETERNAL
LIVING
SOUL

DEATH
(PHYSICAL)

SEPARATION OF THE SOUL FROM THE BODY

WHAT LIFE AND DEATH ARE

UNION
BROKEN

SPIRITUAL DEATH
SEPARATION.

3. SPIRITUAL LIFE
(UNION)

SOUL
BODY

2. PSYCHIC LIFE

1. PHYSICAL LIFE

ALIVE

LESSON 2   The Facts of Life   -- VISUAL AID --

CHAPTER THREE

CHRIST COMING IN THE SPIRIT

REVIEW:

The preceding lesson took us a bit further into God's working with man. The orientation lesson permitted us to view God's overall intention in the earthly program as a testing device for man's will. The last chapter revealed man's eternal soul to be independent of his earthly frame. While his body is earthly and belongs to the physical realm, his soul is unseen and belongs to the spiritual realm. One is temporal; the other is eternal.

We discovered also that God's great passion for man is fired by a consuming longing to have fellowship with Him. Biblically a man is spoken of as dead or alive depending on how he has exercised his free will with regard to God's invitation. If men elect to receive Christ, then they are **united** with God and accepted as spiritually **alive.** If they reject Christ, they remain **separated** from God and are regarded as spiritually **dead.**

We said that God, in order to save man, must do something about man's "nature." By virtue of the fall, man inherited from Adam a nature that is opposed to God. Thus man needs to be equipped with a "new nature" if he is to be eligible as a citizen of heaven. One is not only joined to God, but is instantly equipped with a new nature the moment he receives Christ.

Do you know what this suggests? It means that there is no such thing as death for the Christian. Follow me for just a moment. Since the soul is eternal, man himself cannot really die; he simply shifts from one form of existence into another. There truly is no such thing as death for man as we popularly think of it. Death is something very wonderful; as marvelous as the butterfly emerging from the chrysalis into the glorious winged-state. The fear that natural man has of death shows how his thinking is limited without a knowledge of God's Word. Physical death is but a step in the process, but mankind generally does not know that. He dreads the day when his body will no longer function. He cringes from the blackness of uncertainty that lies ahead. For the Christian, however, it is a different story. The Light of Truth dispels that awful darkness. He sees himself stepping from this life into the sunshine of God's presence.

WHY CHRISTIANITY REALLY SATISFIES

There are many religions in the world today, each claiming to be the only true one. People hear the varied claims and wonder within themselves just which one of them is true and how it may be identified. Their wonderings are understandable. They have secret longings within their souls, yet they hesitate to make a selection from the confused religious scene.

They could be aided, however, by a simple observation. The one who surveys religion notices that they all have one thing in common. They all offer a philosophy; that is, they claim that there is some set of beliefs to which one must subscribe for salvation. They require one to embrace their particular creed. Each religion is certain that it has an approach to God, and if one will live a certain way or do certain things, as well as accept their peculiar doctrine, eventually God will be found in the process — they hope.

When we look at Jesus, we see He is different from all the rest! He dares to do something that none other has ever dared to do. He claims to be God Himself — in the boldest terms, too. He said, "He that hath seen Me hath seen the Father" (John 14:9). When He claims that eternal life is in Him alone — and He does when He says, "I am the truth and the life" (John 14:6) — He sets Himself apart from all religionists. The others claim to **know** the way to God, but Jesus said that He, Himself, **was** the way to God. None other dares to make that claim.

When Jesus claims that eternal life is in Him (John 5:26), He reveals a truth that is unique to Christianity. This truth is not found in any of the religions of the world. So central is this feature to the Christian message, that there is a peculiar sense in which it may be said of Christianity that it is not a religion at all — but a PERSON! Christianity is Christ.

While others insist that one must **believe something** to be saved, our Bible insists that one must **receive someone** in order to have eternal life. Of course, we see the big difference between HAVING the person of Christ and BELIEVING a religious doctrine. One has to do with knowledge; the other, an experience.

Jesus calls our attention to this difference in the eleventh chapter of John where the raising of Lazarus is recorded. Perhaps you are already familiar with the event. Recall the journey that Jesus made to Bethany four days after the death of Lazarus; and how that Martha, the sister of Lazarus, met Him on the outskirts of the city. "Lord," she said to Him, "If Thou hadst been here my brother had not died." (John 11:21). Jesus sought to reassure her, "Thy brother will live again." She answered, "I know that he shall rise in the resurrection . . ." Then Jesus responded with a remarkable lesson for her. It was as though He said to her, "Martha, get your eyes off the **doctrine** of the resurrection and get them on **Me**;" for, and here we quote, "I am the resurrection and the life . . . ." (John 11:25). This verse is familiar to Christians, yet how many have noticed that the resurrection is a **Person**? How many have realized that eternal life is a **Person**? Obviously Martha missed the truth of the doctrine she apparently knew so well.

48

Actually there is no creed or doctrine that can bring life to anyone. No church, or philosophy, or religion of any kind, can save, for salvation is in none of these. The Saviour is a Person, and one must do business with Him, not doctrines. Even the Bible with all its doctrines can save no one, but the Saviour of the Bible can. More than one person has confused the truths of Christ with Christ Himself.

This is what makes Christianity so satisfying. A personal experience with the center of Christianity—an experience with Jesus Christ Himself—actually doing business with a living person. This is the feature that throws the religions of the world into the trash barrel. For regardless of the claims of Mohammed, he is in his tomb today. One can go to where he is buried. The same is true of Confucius and Buddha as well, but there's an **empty** tomb in Palestine today because Christ **arose!** We are actually contemporaneous with the resurrected Christ. The same One who said to His disciples, "I am the Way to God," today knocks at the door of men's hearts everywhere. What a subject this introduces!

GOD'S INGENIOUS METHOD OF PROVIDING SALVATION

Having just considered that Jesus claimed life is in Him personally; we now ask, if this is so, how does one get it? If eternal life is in one man, Christ Jesus, how may other men come to have it? Obviously, they must have Him. Somehow men must come into possession of Christ, if they are to be joined to God. But how is this possible? At first it seems impossible, but deeper investigation reveals the ingenuity of our wonderful God.

When Jesus told His disciples, "I am the Life," He knew men would have to RECEIVE Him in order to

HAVE His life. He knew it required a literal union in order for people to share life with Him. But what a mysterious thing that is. How is it possible for anyone to share Jesus' life with Him?

For such a thing to be possible, it meant that Jesus would **have** to operate differently than He did in the Gospel period. In those days He had a body the same as you and I. He walked about on the earth, confined to His earthly tabernacle, even as we. He was subject to the same physical limitations. He couldn't be two places at the same time. So how was He to come into men's separate lives, as He spoke of doing? Quite obviously the work of bringing salvation to men could not be accomplished as long as He was confined to a body. No, this kind of ministry would have to come **after** He had made a transition from the flesh. Certainly He was available to no one as long as He remained earth-bound.

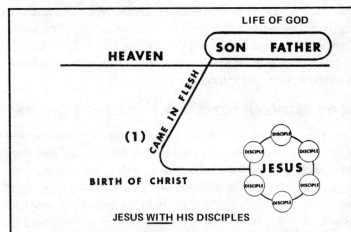

JESUS WITH HIS DISCIPLES

Jesus came to earth and put on a human body to reveal the Father and die on the cross for our sins. Men could see Him and be WITH Him, but the fellowship had to be limited to those close to Him. Obviously there was no way for ALL believers of all ages to have intimate fellowship with Him such as the Bible offers.

As the time of His departure drew near, Jesus began to prepare His disciples and teach them of this deeper truth. The discussion of John fourteen takes place a few hours before the cross. Here He tells them of the "Comforter." He speaks of "another Comforter" (John 14:16) whom He identifies as the Holy Spirit in verse 26. Yet when we look more closely at the verses we find that He is actually referring to Himself.

Verse seventeen allows us to make important observations relative to the "Spirit of Truth." Concerning Him it says," . . . but ye know Him; for He dwelleth **with you,** and shall be **in you.**" From this we learn that the Comforter is someone they **know** who is presently **with** them. This can only be Jesus. He alone is known of them and is with them. When He says, "shall be in you," we are alerted to an important change. Since this is Jesus Himself, He is teaching them that He will undergo a change in FORM as well as **sphere of operation.** As far as identifying Himself as the "Comforter," He does so in the next verse, "I will not leave you comfortless, I WILL COME TO YOU." He is the one who is going to come to them. His identity as the Comforter seems quite clear.

It's not likely that the disciples understood what He meant. There were many things that He taught them which He knew they would not grasp until later. In fact, He mentions from time to time that there are a host of truths which He would love to impart to them, but they are not able to receive them. This truth is certainly a profound one. Many this side of Calvary are "not able to bear it." He assured them, however, that when the "Spirit of Truth" had come He would guide them in their thinking and make His words clear to their hearts (John 16:12-13).

As we move on to verse twenty we find His promise to them that the day of their understanding was not far off.

The day was soon to come when they would know that He was in the Father, they in Him, and **He in them** — the very thing of which He has just been speaking. Without doubt He has been trying to give them some understanding of His future indwelling in their hearts. On a certain day they will know these things are so. That day we know to be the day of Pentecost. That is the day the Comforter came.

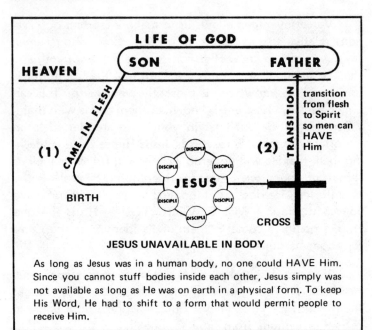

LIFE OF GOD

HEAVEN   SON   FATHER

CAME IN FLESH

(1)   (2)

TRANSITION

transition from flesh to Spirit so men can HAVE Him

JESUS

DISCIPLE DISCIPLE DISCIPLE DISCIPLE DISCIPLE DISCIPLE

BIRTH   CROSS

JESUS UNAVAILABLE IN BODY

As long as Jesus was in a human body, no one could HAVE Him. Since you cannot stuff bodies inside each other, Jesus simply was not available as long as He was on earth in a physical form. To keep His Word, He had to shift to a form that would permit people to receive Him.

Now we're ready to proceed a bit further with our observations. If the Comforter is actually Jesus Himself, coming in the Spirit, then certainly He cannot come as long as He is in a body. The Comforter cannot come until Christ leaves the body. To this Jesus also certifies, "If I go not away the Comforter will not come unto you" (John 16:7). This is another way of saying that as long as He continued to remain with them in the body there was no way possible for them to have eternal life.

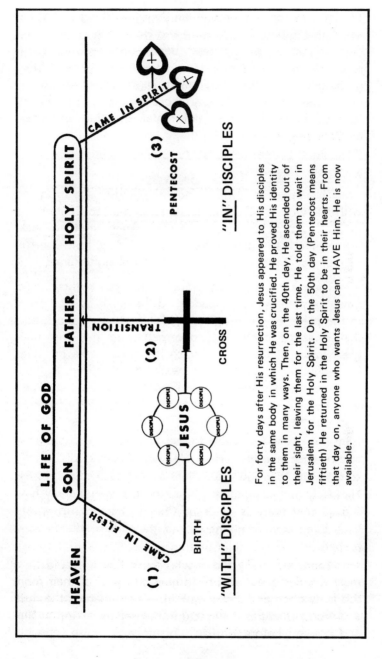

LIFE OF GOD

HEAVEN   SON   FATHER   HOLY SPIRIT

CAME IN FLESH

BIRTH

(1)

"WITH" DISCIPLES

TRANSITION

(2)

CROSS

JESUS — DISCIPLE

CAME IN SPIRIT

PENTECOST

(3)

"IN" DISCIPLES

For forty days after His resurrection, Jesus appeared to His disciples in the same body in which He was crucified. He proved His identity to them in many ways. Then, on the 40th day, He ascended out of their sight, leaving them for the last time. He told them to wait in Jerusalem for the Holy Spirit. On the 50th day (Pentecost means fiftieth) He returned in the Holy Spirit to be in their hearts. From that day on, anyone who wants Jesus can HAVE Him. He is now available.

The words of Jesus suddenly become filled with great meaning when we apprehend this truth. "It is expedient for you that I go away," that is, "it is better for you," or "it is to your advantage for Me to leave you now." They couldn't seem to understand that it was in their best interest that He depart from the world via the cross. He was attempting to convince them that this was the best thing that could happen—not only for them, but for the whole world. If He didn't go men could not have eternal life. Thus it was an absolute necessity.

Those poor little minds, how they must have struggled with His words. Their understanding was so limited and the truth was so big. How gently He dealt with them seeking to give them some understanding, yet the truth was too marvelous. I wonder if we grasp its full significance.

They knew He was going. That much they could grasp very easily, and it saddened them. It grieved them to the place where they had difficulty hearing much else that He said to them. So concerned were they with their great loss that they didn't catch the good news that was hidden in His words. He was aware of their plight, ". . . Because I have said these things unto you, sorrow hath filled your heart." Yet His comfort was the teaching of a new and better relationship that would come as a result of His **transition** from the body to the spirit. How could they realize such a truth. Here He was speaking of actually coming into their individual lives so that each could possess Him fully and completely. Think of it, a man literally having all that there is of Jesus Christ! Indeed this would have been comforting news had they been able to comprehend it.

There are many today who think that it would be a most wonderful experience to have the door of their room suddenly open and Jesus walk in. They imagine the thrill and wonderment as they picture themselves talking to Him and bowing before Him in worship and praise, possibly gazing with tear-filled eyes at the wounds in His hands. As thrilling to contemplate as such a scene might be, what emptiness it would produce were it to happen.

How could His bodily presence begin to compare with His presence in our hearts! If He were here in a body, that is, if He were physically present in the world today a few might get close to Him. Some, perhaps, could embrace Him lovingly, but the great host of Christians could not enjoy His immediate presence. To limit Him to the body-form again would be a terrible loss for us. Mere physical possession of anyone is inadequate, when we think of it.

Your author has a young daughter in whom he delights greatly. There are times, when he holds her in his arms, that he could "eat her up" as the expression goes. She seems so sweet and lovable. All parents have this same experience. You just can't seem to get close enough. The flesh gets in the way. There is no way to **completely** appropriate or enjoy another as long as the flesh separates.

This is what Jesus wanted them to see. He wanted them to know something of the truth of having Him in their hearts. There He would be closer to them than their own hands and nearer than their own breath. This is the preciousness of the indwelling presence of Jesus. Today, when you and I are in trouble, we don't have to spell out our troubles to Jesus with the detailed accuracy of an insurance report. He already knows our hearts. He lives there. This is why He is truly the Comforter.

How wonderful is our salvation when we realize that it comes to us in the person of Jesus. We actually receive the gift of eternal life by **SPECIAL DELIVERY** for the one who died for us brings it to us personally. The Heavenly Messenger brings His own work for us, accomplished at Calvary, right into our hearts. Jesus was not satisfied simply to die for us, He wants to see that the benefit of His work is carried out in our lives. So it is that He brings His redemptive work to each of us personally. He remains with us to insure and guarantee that nothing can possibly go wrong with it. How dear are His words, "When He is come, He will abide **forever**" (John 14:16). The Comforter, (a new name for Jesus' spirit-ministry) is to abide with us forever. Even now I know that some of you dear readers are tempted to ask, "How can these things be?"

HOW IS THIS LITERAL WORKING IN OUR LIVES POSSIBLE?

When we say that a person literally comes into men's hearts and lives, questions automatically present themselves. How can He, who is but one person, be in all of our hearts at the same time? And secondly, how does the cross, an event which took place 2000 years ago, have anything to do with men today?

We are in a much better position to understand the presence of Jesus in our lives than were the disciples. The reason is because we have television. Does this surprise you? It is one of the best aids to understanding this mystery. Television, itself, is something of a miracle. Certainly it would appear miraculous to Peter and John—every bit as much as did Jesus' walking on the water. When we understand something of this modern miracle, we are in a position to comprehend the mystery of Christ's indwelling.

What we say concerning television, please remember, is simply by way of illustration. The analogy will not carry all the way.

56

In an oversimplified explanation of television operation, we find a scene takes place in a studio. By means of a transmitter it is sent out over television waves to the surrounding area. Anyone with a television receiver is able to pick up those waves and have a reproduced image on his own T.V. screen. The very scene of the studio is now transferred to his home. Not only is the scene reproduced in just one home, but in as many as **will receive** it. There is no limit to the number of sets that can receive the image from the studio; in fact, "whosoever will" may turn his set to the channel and receive what is offered.

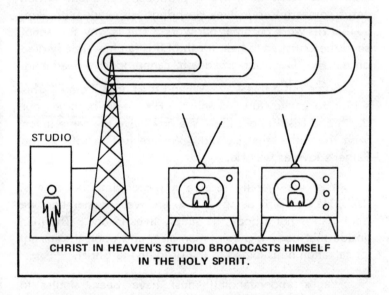

CHRIST IN HEAVEN'S STUDIO BROADCASTS HIMSELF IN THE HOLY SPIRIT.

If men can reproduce a scene, which takes place in a distant studio, in a multitude of homes, surely Jesus can reproduce His presence in as many lives as will receive Him. In a peculiar sense the Holy Spirit may be likened to the transmitting waves so that the image that is formed in us is Jesus. We become receiving sets for the divine Transmitter. In this way we receive the Lord completely, and there is no limit to the number who are invited to do so. God would have every man tune himself to station J-E-S-U-S.

Sometimes people confess difficulty in relating the cross to their personal lives. They ask, "What does the cross have to do with me here in the Twentieth Century?"

It would be difficult to see if one separated the cross from Christ. Actually, however, the cross itself has nothing to do with us, but the death that was accomplished there does. We are joined to the One who died there. Thus the answer to the question is this; what Jesus did **for** us two thousand years ago, He does **in** us today. His cross made salvation **possible**, His Spirit-ministry makes salvation **available**. His work at Calvary produced salvation. When Jesus comes into our lives He brings His work with Him, so that **His** work becomes **our** work. This is why sin cannot send the Christian to hell, for the Christian has already died once. The "law of sin and death" cannot touch a dead man.

Some put it this way, "When Christ died, I died." This serves to convey our meaning. His **death** becomes our death and His **life**, our life. We now have the same union with the Father that He did. We are just as safe in the Father's love as was He.

Yes, we literally receive a person into our hearts. True, He's a spirit being, but so are we. Remember, we said man is not a body, he simply lives in one. The man inside that body is a spirit-man also, and upon the instant of salvation he is joined to the risen, living Christ.

Paul's understanding must have been similar to this. In one place he remarks, ". . . which is Christ **in** you, the hope of glory" (Col. 1:27), in another, "As ye have therefore **received** Christ Jesus . . ." (Col. 2:6), or again, "That Christ may **dwell** in your hearts by faith" (Eph. 3:17).

This is also why the apostle John insists that, "He that **hath** (has) the Son, hath life, and he that **hath not** the Son hath not life" (I John 5:12). As far as the devoted apostle was concerned, there were only two classes of people; those that had Christ and those who didn't. The world recognizes the "have's" and "have-nots," apparently God does too.

This is why we, as soul-winners, give the New Testament invitation when dealing with unsaved ones, "Behold I stand at the door and knock, if any man hear My voice and open the door, I WILL COME IN . . ." (Rev. 3:20). We do not hesitate to tell men that if they will open their heart's door, Christ will come in. We know that He will. He has come into our own lives. We know too, that the promise He made to His disciples just before the cross, He kept. This blessed and glorious person does actually come into our lives bringing the work of His cross by SPECIAL DELIVERY!

CHRIST COMING IN THE SPIRIT

MAIN TEACHING (Review and Remember)

1. Eternal life is union with the person of God.

2. Jesus was God, come in the flesh, bringing eternal life to men (John 5:26).

3. As long as Jesus was in the body His life (union) was not available to men. He, Himself, was not in an available form.

4. Before His death He told the disciples that He would come again in the Spirit, then each, who wanted Him, could receive Him personally.

5. At the cross Jesus makes a transition from the body ministry to the Spirit. His body was necessary for the priestly atoning ministries.

6. His atoning work was finished at Calvary and Jesus began His work of coming in the Spirit. This actually began on the day of Pentecost.

7. Now each person can have eternal life, because Christ is in an **available form**. Now He is the omnipresent Spirit and can be received by anyone.

8. How each one can have all of Christ is illustrated by modern television transmission. The main scene takes place in the studio (heaven) and the image is beamed via radio waves (The Holy Spirit) with the image being reproduced in each receiver (the believer). There is no limit to the number who can receive Christ in this way.

9. The death of Christ is **FOR** all men, but it is by the

Holy Spirit that it becomes **AVAILABLE** to all men. Each, who receives Christ personally, receives His two-fold death to sin and life unto God.

10. What Jesus did **FOR** us at Calvary, the Holy Spirit does **IN** us when we make the decision to open the door of our hearts to the Lord.

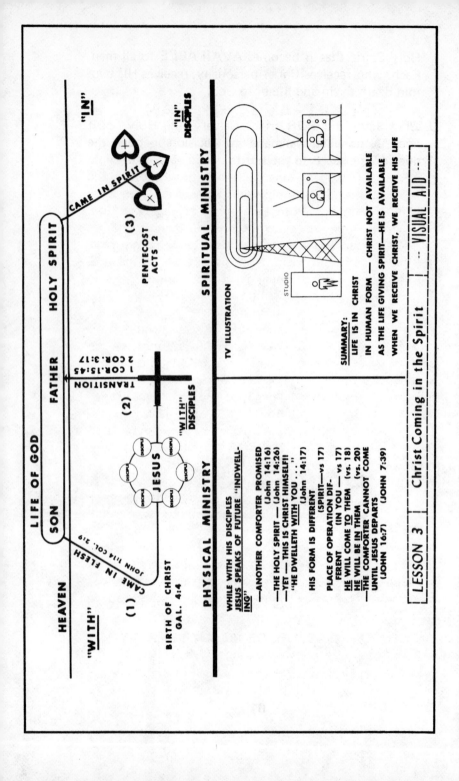

LIFE OF GOD

HEAVEN   SON   FATHER   HOLY SPIRIT   "IN"

"WITH"

CAME IN FLESH
JOHN 1:14 COL. 2:9

(1)

BIRTH OF CHRIST
GAL. 4:4

TRANSITION
1 COR. 15:45
2 COR. 3:17

(2)

"WITH"
DISCIPLES

JESUS
(DISCIPLE × 8)

CAME IN SPIRIT

(3)

PENTECOST
ACTS 2

"IN"
DISCIPLES

PHYSICAL MINISTRY

WHILE WITH HIS DISCIPLES
JESUS SPEAKS OF FUTURE "INDWELL-
ING"

—ANOTHER COMFORTER PROMISED
         (John 14:16)
—THE HOLY SPIRIT — (John 14:26)
—YET — THIS IS CHRIST HIMSELF!!
        "HE DWELLETH WITH YOU . . ."
                    (John 14:17)

HIS FORM IS DIFFERENT
                    (SPIRIT—vs 17)
PLACE OF OPERATION DIF-
FERENT   (IN YOU — vs 17)
HE WILL COME TO THEM (vs. 18)
HE WILL BE IN THEM   (vs. 20)
—THE COMFORTER CANNOT COME
UNTIL JESUS DEPARTS
    (JOHN 16:7) (JOHN 7:39)

SPIRITUAL MINISTRY

TV ILLUSTRATION

STUDIO

SUMMARY:
LIFE IS IN CHRIST
IN HUMAN FORM — CHRIST NOT AVAILABLE
AS THE LIFE GIVING SPIRIT—HE IS AVAILABLE
WHEN WE RECEIVE CHRIST, WE RECEIVE HIS LIFE

-- VISUAL AID --

| LESSON 3 | Christ Coming in the Spirit |

CHAPTER FOUR

THE DEPRAVITY OF MAN

The outstanding feature of our 2nd chapter was the fact that God made man in His own image so that He might enjoy him. God made man so that He could prepare and look forward to a fellowship with those of His own kind. Men need fellowship with each other, so also does God. He is a person and can enjoy those of His own in kind.

While men enjoy animals as pets, they cannot have true fellowship with them. Animals operate by instincts. We, by virtue of our intelligence and reason, require companionship with those on our own level. God does, too. Because we are made in His image, we are able to supply Him with satisfying companionship.

We noted also that true fellowship requires man to be possessed of a free will, and like God, able to determine his own destiny. Interaction and response are needed for fellowship. The relationship that God has in mind is likened to that of a father to his children, and the love exchanged is of the same order. Love, itself, is a free act of the will. Anything less would be too machine-like to be satisfying to God.

Beyond this, we learned the whole of human history and life on this earth, as we know it, is a testing for man's free will. Man's will needs to be exercised either in behalf of God or against Him before he can enter the final state. Man needs an opportunity to determine for himself where he will spend eternity and with whom. Thus all of life, as we know life, is temporary. Even the jagged cliffs of our mountains wear away. The sun, too, is scheduled to burn to extinction.

THE SOURCE AND CAUSE OF HUMAN DEPRAVITY

Before we can deal with the subject of man's depravity, we need to investigate further the image of God. We need to know more about that image. Why? Depravity has its source in man's nature. Recall that we said God's program of redemption has to deal with man's nature for that is the point at which God and man are separated.

To learn of this, we return to the second chapter of Genesis and re-examine the verse which told us of man's formation. This time we look more closely. "God **FORMED** man out of the dust." The forming from the dust has reference to Adam's body. It is that part of man which is composed of earthly elements. Then we move on, ". . . and **BREATHED** in his nostrils the breath of life." This breath, which we previously observed as giving Adam his life, may now be more narrowly defined. This we shall describe as his **spirit**, or as referred to later as the "spirit of man" (I Cor. 2:11).

There's a third and important thing to be noted. Something else happened to Adam, ". . . and man **BECAME A LIVING SOUL**." This is the man himself. Adam was not a body. He had a body, and also a spirit, but he himself was a living soul. Thus we find man to be a tripartite being. There are three elements in the makeup of **earthly** man — body, soul, and spirit. Paul makes this distinction in giving his benediction to the Thessalonians, ". . . And I pray God your whole SPIRIT and SOUL and BODY be preserved blameless unto the coming of our Lord Jesus Christ " (I Thess. 5:23).

The writer to the Hebrews adds his testimony to this truth. He says the "Word of God" able to divide assunder the "soul and the spirit" (Heb. 4:12). Even though we have noted these distinctions within the make up of man, we are always careful to state that man **is** a soul. He is a person, but **possessed** of a body and spirit.

The soul, or the person, is the image of God. This must be clear in our minds. He is the creation that God made for Himself and loves so desperately. The spirit of man is that which gives to him his personality. Yet it is so related to the soul as to affect his thinking and behavior.

The soul, because of the spirit, presents a distinct personality. There are some finer points which theologians and psychologists like to debate, but this is sufficiently accurate for our teaching. Finally, the body serves merely to **house** the person and **reveal** his personality. Thus earthly man's three components are body, soul, and spirit.

A man cannot be seen. All anyone can behold of another person is that which is manifested by means of the physical body. The inner person is spirit and hence invisible. The thinking process cannot be observed. No one has ever seen a man's thoughts. He may offer a penny to hear them, but he cannot see them. Neither are his loves or hatreds visible. What is known of any person is that revealed by words and deeds. Even these have to be interpreted by others. The pictures that are formed in people's minds, as they view others, are all different. We will never really see each other until the day when all of us put off the mask of the flesh and stand before God in the spirit.

The first man, Adam, was a soul. Fresh from the hand of God he was pure. He had no sin. This is not to say that he was perfect or righteous, but only that he was innocent. He was not guilty of any transgression of God's revealed will which simply means he was innocent.

Adam remained innocent until he committed some overt freewill act that was opposed to God's desire for him. As long as he was innocent, he could enjoy the presence of the Lord. Yet, because Adam was innocent and in fellowship with God does not mean that he was righteous. Adam's righteousness was something that had to be determined — determined and produced by his obedience. Adam was not created a righteous man as is sometimes believed. He was innocent yes, but innocence and righteousness are not the same.

The noted theologian, Fairbairn, makes a helpful observation at this point:

65

Moral perfection can be attained, that is, acquired, but it cannot be created. God can make a being capable of moral action, but not a being with all of the fruits of moral action garnered within him.

In other words, God could make Adam capable of doing righteously, but not so that he couldn't do wrongly. Adam must be capable of both right and wrong. There is no way to guarantee what any freewill creature will do.

Obviously Adam was not perfect or he would not have sinned. His own disobedience declared him to be imperfect. It is impossible to make any freewill agent morally perfect. Perfection means that a man will **always** choose to do right when faced with wrong. He must, at the same time, be able to **choose** between right and wrong and **capable** of doing either. A man is perfect, when capable of doing either right or wrong, he freely elects to do good only. Adam did not qualify as a perfect man.

The best that we can say of Adam, before the fall, was that he was innocent. His righteousness had yet to be determined. As a freewill being his destiny and moral character were in his own hands. In fact, his **nature** was in his own hands, too. If he chose to do **only** those things which were pleasing in the sight of God, then he would produce a righteous nature. If he freely elected to do otherwise, he would produce for himself an unrighteous nature.

 Adam had but a single test, the "tree." It stood there in the midst of the garden day after day. No doubt every time Adam looked at it he was reminded of God's instructions, "But of the tree containing the knowledge of good and evil, thou shalt not eat of it. . ." For the most part Adam was very happy to do the will of God. The tree, as it

stood there, was not much of a threat to his peace of mind. But on that fateful day when Satan successfully deceived Eve, Adam suddenly became vulnerable.

The pressure of those moments must have been terrific! It was more than the simple question of whether or not to eat some fruit. It was whether he would now obey God or Satan. Adam knew full well what was going on. You can be sure he debated his decision with collected calm. Paul teaches us this when he tells Timothy that "Adam was not deceived" (I Tim. 2:14). Adam was aware of the consequences too, for God had fully instructed him. Now, what would he do? To whom would he surrender, God or Satan? That was his real problem.

Whichever way Adam decided would determine his nature or personality. If he chose to obey God, then he would acquire a nature that wanted only to please the Lord. If, instead, he chose to obey Satan, the resulting nature would be one opposed to God. Adam's future and humanity's nature stood in the balance awaiting his decision.

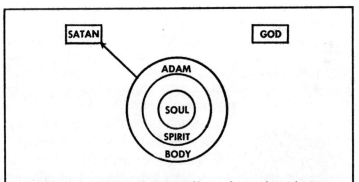

Adam was in the valley of decision. He was free to choose between God and Satan. Whichever choice he made would determine his nature. As yet his nature was neither righteous nor unrighteous, but innocent. His choice to please Satan gave him a Satan-pleasing (self-centered) nature. Now he was controlled by an anti-God and pro-Satan nature.

When Adam elected to please Satan rather than God, he threw away his opportunity to be perfect and acquire a godly character. In that same instant his nature assumed its set. Now he had a God-opposed nature. His spirit became subject to Satan, and Adam entered into a bondage from which he would have to be redeemed. If not, God could never enjoy him again.

The soul of Adam, that is, Adam in his **being,** remained as the image of God. But now that image was possessed of a fallen spirit. The spirit that now motivated Adam was opposed to God who had made him. All of Adam's choices and acts now would be directed by self-centered thinking. Self-centeredness is the outstanding feature of a Satan-controlled life. Adam was willingly bound to Satan by **nature.**

What a loss to God. The soul that He had created for Himself had willingly given himself over to that rebel, Satan. Now His creation was directed by the "Prince of the power of the air." Adam was the devil's bondslave; captive because of his unrighteous nature. No longer was he the servant of God.

That wasn't all God lost that day. Through this one man's decision, all men who were to come after Adam were also lost to Him. When Satan got the first pair, he got the whole of mankind. Adam's heirs could receive from him only what he had to pass on, and that was an unrighteous nature. God's own law of the harvest had to stand; like begets like. Sinners can only produce sinners. Adam and Eve by their own choices were now sinners. Their offspring could only be sinners as well.

 Adam's fall produced an ungodly, rebellious nature. This is the only nature he had to pass on to his heirs. So it was that mankind fell into bondage. The spirit of man which Adam was supposed to develop into

Godlikeness, became the "spirit of bondage," as Paul calls it (Rom. 8:15a). Everyone descended from Adam receives this nature which is opposed to God. Every person born in the line of Adam is dominated by this fallen nature.

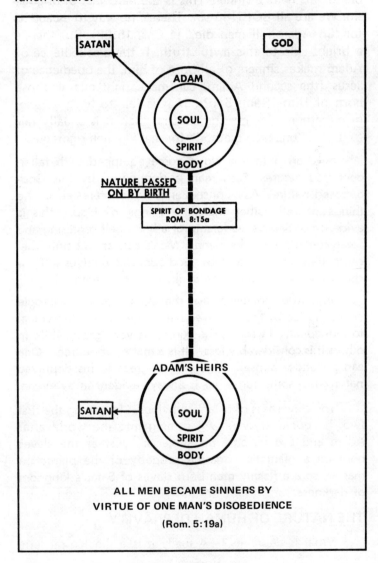

NATURE PASSED ON BY BIRTH

SPIRIT OF BONDAGE ROM. 8:15a

SATAN

GOD

ADAM

SOUL

SPIRIT

BODY

ADAM'S HEIRS

SATAN

SOUL

SPIRIT

BODY

ALL MEN BECAME SINNERS BY VIRTUE OF ONE MAN'S DISOBEDIENCE

(Rom. 5:19a)

When Adam defied God in the garden, he made sinners of all of us. "It was through one man," says the apostle Paul, "that sin entered the world" (Rom. 5:12). When the father of the human race sinned, he made every one of his heirs a sinner. This is the hard fact of original sin. We are all BORN in sin. There's no way to escape it, for "in Adam, all men die" (1 Cor. 15:22). But there's a bright side to this awful truth. If the disobedience of Adam makes sinners of all born of him, the obedience of Jesus (the second Adam) can make righteous all those born of Him (Rom. 5:19). If it is fair to have a "one-man-method" for making sinners, then it is equally fair to have a "one-Man-method" for making men righteous.

All born into this world come equipped with fallen depraved natures. Each man is dominated by this God-opposed nature. As a consequence he is interested in the things of self rather than the things of God. This is evidence of Satan's leadership of a life. Self-centering and Satan-centering are the same. Men's acts are all sinful because they are directed by God-opposed motives. Their choices are sinful inasmuch as they are self-centered.

It is true, however, that the extent to which people are controlled by the depraved nature varies from individual to individual. In some, the control is very great while in others it is considerably less. It is a matter of degree. One can surrender himself in varying degrees to his depraved nature, but some surrender is always evident in everyone.

The cleverness of Satan is obvious. In getting the first two, he got everyone. All coming into the world after Adam and Eve become his subjects. Just as the slaves born on a plantation are the property of the plantation master, so are fleshly men born slaves of Satan's kingdom of darkness.

THE NATURE OF HUMAN DEPRAVITY

What is depravity? Actually it is a theological term

that refers to man's natural state. Specifically, it has in mind the bondage to the fallen, unholy spirit that is within man. Bondage to the "spirit of man" prevents one from pleasing God. By definition, the depraved man is one who is possessed of but one nature, and that **nature** is contrary to God.

It does not mean that a man is one hundred percent wicked, as we think of wickedness popularly. It does not mean that depraved men are all wife-beaters and murderers. The popular idea of depravity is largely in terms of sadists and homosexuals; but biblically, depravity does not mean this at all. It's primary reference is to man's inability to do **anything** to make himself right with God.

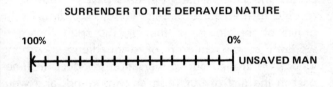

SURRENDER TO THE DEPRAVED NATURE

100%　　　　　　　　　　　　0%　　　　UNSAVED MAN

Because a man has a fallen nature does not mean he will be totally bad. He still has a free will. He can resist the ungodly impulses that surge within him. This is why some people appear to be good and others bad. Every unsaved person is somewhere on a scale of zero to a hundred percent surrender to his fallen nature.

All mankind is in this depraved condition, even those who are good husbands and wives and well thought of. They may hold high offices in our land. They may be the mayors of our cities and the most respected churchgoers. They may even live lives that surpass those of most profess-ing Christians, but they are depraved if they are unsaved.

Many think that "skid row" is the devil's idea. Why, he hates that worse than we do. Men, who are down and out, are susceptible to the "Good News," just as the misera-bles throughout the world are susceptible to Communism's promise of prosperity. Satan prefers that men live in nice homes enjoying the good things of life. They are far less vulnerable to the Christian message when satisfied with their lot. A busy life that is sociable and respected is more to Satan's liking.

We need to keep in mind that depravity is man's natural state of opposition to God — the state into which each of us is born by virtue of his descent from Adam. The nature of man seeks to dominate him, and behind that nature are the wily suggestions of the "evil one" himself. So complete is man's bondage that the Bible has some very striking things to say about it. Paul's language to the Ephesians is addressed to this point:

> And you hath he quickened who were **dead** in trespasses and sins: wherein in **time past** ye walked according to the course of this world, according to the prince of the power of the air, the **spirit** that now worketh in the children of disobedience: Among whom we **all** had our conversation (conduct) in times past in the lust of our flesh and the mind, and were **by nature** the children of wrath, even as others. (Eph. 2:1-3)

Other places describe men in bondage as "captives of Satan" or "slaves to sin." A further commentary on the Word says that depraved men, "cannot receive the truth," "cannot believe," "they cannot please God," and neither can they come to Christ.

Certainly the Bible views depraved men as hopelessly and helplessly meshed in their bondage. As such they are lost to God. Their acts, because they are not "of faith," must be classed as sin. Separated from God, they must remain "dead in trespasses and sins" unless somehow redeemed. There is no fellowship with God for now He is resisted and resented. God will not enter into man's depravity with him for the sake of fellowship; His holiness would not consent to such a thing. No, man's depravity

72

must be dealt with before the creation can be restored to its Maker.

GOD'S ANSWER TO HUMAN DEPRAVITY

Instead of abandoning the human experiment, God makes unique provision for man's restoration to Himself. God loves man (the soul), who is made in His image, and has a great longing to bring him back into fellowship. But to do this, man has to be set free from the God-opposing nature that binds him. Quite obviously this is something that man cannot do for himself. Therefore God must do it for him. Man's help must come from outside.

Yet even though God is ready to minister His great power in behalf of man, it has to be done in a way that is consistent with man's human freedom. Whatever attempt is made has to be on the basis of man's freewill response for that is what God seeks. To change man's nature against his will would be a violation of his sovereignty and nullify the very thing that God wants from man. Any approach must consider that man is a FREEWILL BEING.

Man's nature is the trouble spot — that is clear. This unholy disposition has to be dealt with or there can be no redemption. Something has to offset or counteract the unholy spirit in man. Instantly the answer comes to us: the Holy Spirit. What a staggering thing this is. God offering to men the HOLY Spirit as a gift. Surely it has to be a gift, for what man is worthy to receive the Holy One. How sublime, then, are the words, ". . . how much more shall your heavenly Father **give** the Holy Spirit to them that **ask** Him" (Luke 11:13).

But this raises a problem. How can man, who is depraved, ask for the Holy Spirit? How can he receive the gift of the Holy Spirit? If man is dominated by a nature which is opposed to God's desires, how can he receive the gift? Obviously something else has to be done for man. His bondage must be dealt with in some way so that he

73

can receive the gift. This is the last thing in the world a Satan-inspired unholy spirit would allow him to do. What is the divine answer?

Here is the answer. There is a working of the Holy Spirit in men **before** salvation. This working we call PRE-SALVATION ILLUMINATION. This is an unemphasized subject. The Holy Spirit has a ministry to all men. Everyone, saved and unsaved alike, receives of the grace of God in this way. He loves all men without distinction.

First, there is the conviction of sin. "And when He is come He will reprove the world (not just Christians) of sin," said Jesus in speaking of the Spirit's ministry. (John 16:8). This is the real reason why men are religious. Everywhere people worship something, even if it is the sun or a tree. They do this because they are convicted of sin.

Secondly, the Holy Spirit convicts men of their **need** of salvation. They are unconsciously aware of their need to be delivered from sin. All men feel that somehow they must come into a right relationship with their god. Most, however, pervert the true witness of the Holy Spirit and try to placate this conviction with offerings, rituals, and some kind of works. By the Spirit's working, men are made aware that they are responsible for their deeds and their hearts burn with uneasiness. This is why the man in the foxhole cries out when he suspects his end is at hand. He instinctively fears the impending judgment.

Thirdly, the Holy Spirit reveals Christ as the only Saviour. This is not to say that all men have an awareness that Jesus is the Way to God — most do not. It is most evident that the Spirit's witness to this truth is refused generally. PRE-SALVATION ILLUMINATION is by grace. At no point is the Spirit's work jammed down men's throats. They are always free to take or leave any of God's appeals.

A fourth working of the Holy Spirit is necessary before salvation can occur. For those who have accepted the first

74

three features of the Spirit's witness, there comes another. This last is all important. Here they receive from Him the POWER to make a decision for Christ. This is something that they could not do otherwise. Their **depravity** would not permit it.

Here then are the four steps:

1. The conviction of sin.
2. The conviction of the need of salvation.
3. The revealing of Christ as the only Saviour.
4. The granting of power to decide for Christ.

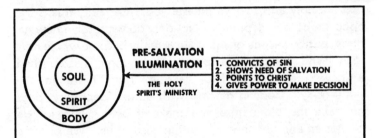

See how the depraved man, trapped in the "spirit of bondage," can do NONE of these things for himself. He has to receive help from God. Yet at no point is his freedom of choice ever violated. While God takes the initiative to rescue lost man, His efforts can be refused. God will not overrule human freedom. He desires man's FREEWILL response to His wooing. Nothing less will give Him what He wants. We were created for fellowship, not servitude.

When men go to hell it is because they have spurned the gift of God. None can ever say that God sent him there. He sent himself. No one ever goes to hell because God wants him there, but only because he elects to go. God "would have none to perish," but His will is not **forcibly** carried out. Hence, most men do perish in spite of all that God does to prevent it. In the face of God's yearning for them, they "prefer darkness rather than light" and bring their own condemnation.

THE RECEIPT OF THE NEW NATURE

When men receive the Holy Spirit something wonderful happens. The high point of the last chapter comes back into view. When we receive the Holy Spirit, we are actually receiving the "Spirit of Christ." Not only does the Spirit of God work in us to overcome our depravity so that we can make a decision for Jesus, but the instant we do, He comes into our hearts. He first enables our decision. Then we freely and literally receive Him.

In the same moment a new nature is established within us. We become the "sons of God" and acquire natures that are holy and seek to please God. Certainly this is the opposite of our depravity. Not only do we receive new natures, but by means of them we actually become whole new men. With receipt of the Spirit of Christ, there is established a "new creation," as Paul calls it, right there in the same body. God, in dealing with human depravity, does not take the old nature and make it over. Instead, He creates an entirely new one within each of us. We become new creatures or new men.

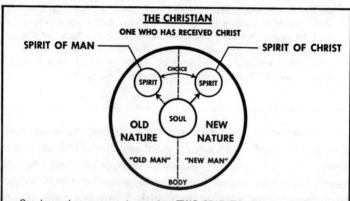

THE CHRISTIAN
ONE WHO HAS RECEIVED CHRIST

SPIRIT OF MAN — SPIRIT OF CHRIST

CHOICE

SPIRIT   SPIRIT

SOUL

OLD NATURE   NEW NATURE

"OLD MAN"   "NEW MAN"

BODY

See how the same soul now has TWO SPIRITS—the spirit of man and the Spirit of Christ. The body, soul, and Spirit of Christ constitute the "new creation." It is as though the "old man" has moved over to make room for the "new man," so that the two dwell side by side in the one body.

The new man occupies the same body along with the old man. They coexist side by side. Each has the full compliment of body, soul and spirit. The body, soul and "spirit of man" constitute the OLD MAN. **He remains unchanged.** The same body, same soul and the "Spirit of Christ" make up the NEW MAN. He is the new creation of God that occurs upon salvation. The receipt of the Holy Spirit makes it possible to have two men within the one body. The soul of man now has a new Spirit from God which can dominate him, and the soul will therefore exhibit an entirely new personality. Remember we said that the spirit of a man gives him his personality.

The creation of the NEW MAN within us is the true meaning of the expression "born again" or, "Born of the Spirit." While it is the same soul, a whole new personality comes into being. Let me emphasize again that nothing happens to the soul in salvation. Nothing happened to Adam's soul at the fall. That is, no change took place within the soul itself. The control of that soul changed hands. Both in salvation and the fall, the issue is one of the direction in which the soul is headed and to whom it is joined. The soul remains forever the image of God.

One might ask, "How does receiving the Spirit of God give us a God-pleasing nature? If, as we have said, a nature has to be produced by a life, just where does this new nature acquire its righteousness?"

The question brings us to a thrilling truth, one which will be explored further as we move into the other lessons. Our answer is that it comes from the "Second Adam." Our Lord Jesus, who is referred to as the Second Adam, was tested just like the first Adam. His testing ended in victory instead of failure. His victorious life produced a holy and righteous nature. That nature is passed on to His heirs, those born of Him, just as Adam's nature was passed on to those born of him. One is a birth of the "flesh;" the other, of the "Spirit."

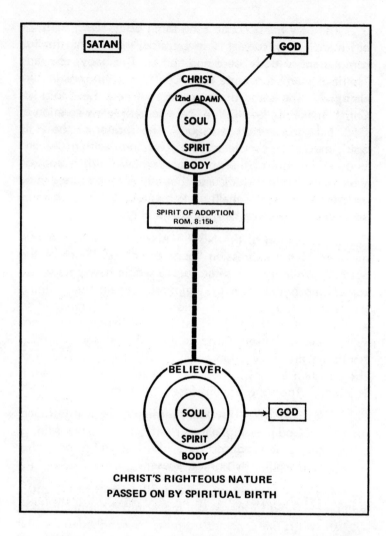

CHRIST'S RIGHTEOUS NATURE
PASSED ON BY SPIRITUAL BIRTH

When a man is born of Christ, he becomes a partaker of Christ's own nature — His **sinless** nature   (2 Peter 1:4). What a wonderful thing to happen to a depraved human! Now we have natures that are righteous and which cannot sin.   Natures, which if allowed to **fully** control us, would cause us to please God continually.   Oh, if that were only so in experience!

Here we must notice something important. To miss it will cause trouble in understanding God's dealing with us. Once we become the "sons of God" through this new creation, we are **FREE** from the old bondage, but not **RID** of it. Having the new nature makes it **possible** for us to live a God-pleasing life, but it is **no guarantee** that we will. It simply means that we do not have to submit to the unrighteous demands of the old man any longer—if we don't want to. We are loosed from sin's continual domination of our lives and are free to please God by submitting to the new nature, IF WE WANT TO. Remember God never forces anything on us—ever.

SUMMARY

This has been a big lesson. The truths will be encountered again before the course is ended. The main things to observe are:

1. The tripartite formation of man and why the original creation was **neutral** in nature.

2. Adam's surrender to Satan which produced a depraved nature that resulted in man's bondage and separation from God.

3. God moves toward all men to set them free from their bondage by means of PRE-SALVATION ILLUMINATION. In no way does it violate their freedom of choice.

4. Receiving the "Spirit of Christ" establishes a new nature within the person and permits him to please God and fellowship with Him.

5. The new nature is God's answer to human depravity.

79

THE DEPRAVITY OF MAN

MAIN TEACHING (Review and Remember)

1. Adam was created tripartite: body, soul, and spirit (Gen. 2:7).

2. Adam's free will was tested (tree) and he became a sinner by choosing to please self (Satan) rather than God. Until this act, Adam was innocent and fellowshipped with God.

3. In surrendering his spirit, Adam acquired a corrupt nature which he passed to all his heirs.

4. This produced human depravity which makes all men sinners and alienated from God. All of us sinned when Adam sinned. (Rom. 5:12)

5. God must free man from this bondage if there is to be any future fellowship.

6. God aids man by means of Pre-Salvation Illumination. This process, which never interferes with man's free will, does four things for him:

    a. brings conviction of sin
    b. shows the need of a Savior
    c. reveals Christ as only Savior
    d. grants power for decision

7. Upon his decision a man receives the Holy Spirit and becomes a son of God.

8. The second birth brings men a new nature which is inherited from the Second Adam (Christ).

9. Equipped with a new nature inherited from Christ, man can now please God and is eligible for heaven's fellowship.

10. Depravity is overcome for now man is free to please God if he wants to. It is the new nature that makes it possible.

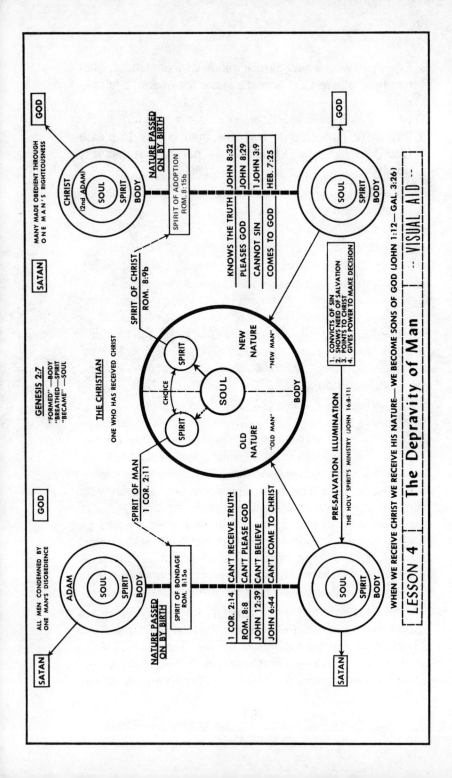

LESSON 4 — The Depravity of Man — VISUAL AID

CHAPTER FIVE

THE TWO NATURES OF THE BELIEVER

In the last chapter, we investigated for the second time the truths of man's structure as set forth in Genesis 2:7. While we have declared man to be a soul, we noted that he is also possessed of a body and spirit. These three features combine to make up earthly man as we know him.

The **nature** of man was something that had to be determined by man himself. For this to be accomplished Adam, the first man, was created innocent and capable of either righteous or unrighteous acts. By his own free choice to please Satan rather than God, Adam acquired a depraved nature. His God-opposing nature and the tendency to sin was passed on to all of his heirs so that each man born into the world enters equipped with an unrighteous nature of his own.

The choices of all men after Adam are evil. Thus they become sinners in their own right; their sin being a "by-product" of their own depraved natures. Through the tragedy of the fall, the control of mankind passed into the hands of Satan. All men are identified with him as slaves born into his dark kingdom. Ephesians tells us that they are "by nature the children of wrath." So depraved are they that they cannot please God; they cannot come to God; they cannot believe or receive the truth; and neither can they cease from sin. They are in a bondage from which there is no escape unless help comes from the outside. Something has to be done about the fallen nature.

We learned that the first step in God's answer to human depravity was **pre-salvation illumination**. This is an illumination that comes before one is saved. The Holy Spirit works in unregenerate man to convict him of his sin and need of salvation, as well as giving him the power to receive Christ. Upon the instant of decision, the "Spirit of Christ" enters the believer and a new nature is created.

THE STRUCTURE OF THE BELIEVER

As we learned from lesson three, we literally receive Christ in the Spirit. A glance at our visual below pictures for us the structure of the believer now that he has received the Spirit of God. He is different from the natural man in that he possesses two natures instead of one. We note, however, that the believer has the very same body that he had before he was saved. No change occurs within his soul either. He is the same soul and remains the image of God. Even the same "spirit of man" is still there, to make up a complete "old man" — the same old nature which formerly made the soul a slave of Satan.

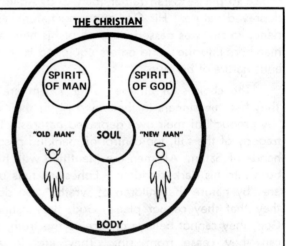

THE CHRISTIAN

SPIRIT OF MAN — SPIRIT OF GOD — "OLD MAN" — SOUL — "NEW MAN" — BODY

From the drawing you can see how it is impossible to be saved apart from receiving the Spirit of God. There can be no new nature without the Holy Spirit. Inasmuch as this Spirit is HOLY, the new nature is holy also. It is the receipt of a holy nature that makes it possible for a person to grow in holiness and live in the presence of a holy God. No one can go to heaven without it. Yet we need to see that it is the SOUL that develops in holiness, not the person's nature. It is already holy. It is the man who develops.

Having the Holy Spirit, however, causes a marvelous miracle to take place. The body and the soul unite with the newly received "Spirit of God" to form a complete new man. Remember we said that it takes these three elements to make a man. Well, here they are. This time they form a new man and the soul is equipped with a new nature. The body, soul and "spirit of man" still combine to make up the "old man;" and the body, soul and "Spirit of Christ" combine to form the "new man." Thus we have **two men occupying the same body.** The difference between the two men is one of spirit. "The spirit of man" produces the God-opposing nature, and the "Spirit of Christ" produces the God-pleasing nature.

No man can have the new nature unless he has the Spirit of God. This is the way that men are joined to God; they actually receive Christ in the Spirit. A man is saved by receiving Christ in this way; for as Paul notes, "If any man have not the Spirit of Christ, he is none of His" (Rom. 8:9). John adds a further word in His first Epistle, "Hereby we know that He abides in us by His Spirit which He has given us." We know that Christ lives in our hearts because we have received the Spirit which is of God. His Spirit testifies to us that we belong to God; or as certified in another place, "He that believeth on the Son of God hath the witness in himself . . ." (1st John 5:10)

The soul of man is the image of God. It is controlled by one nature only before salvation, and is separated from God by virtue of the sin which is produced by that Satan-dominated nature. The spirit of man is accurately described as "the spirit of bondage." It is the matter of spirit-control that makes the difference between a child of God and a child of the devil. The eternal soul is joined to God when the person opens his heart to Jesus. Now the believer possesses another Spirit which seeks to bring him under the influence of Christ. This Spirit is accurately described as "the Spirit of Adoption" or Sonship (Rom. 8:15). Thus it is that the believer has two natures which are the products of two spirits. The soul does not change. He will always be the **same person** regardless of any change in nature.

Note: Let me mention something that can be confusing. We have said that a man's soul and his spirit are two separate things. Yet both of them are spirit. Now that's not double-talk. I mean both of them are made of spirit, that's their raw essence. After all, God is Spirit (John 4:24). Therefore, His image (man's soul) has to be spirit also. The soul is the EGO, the self-conscious person who thinks and feels and decides. But he has a spirit, an accessory that feeds impulses which stimulate him. That accessory is the "spirit of man." It works like a radio station designed to pick up only one station. Unfortunately man's spirit is tuned to station S-A-T-A-N. Adam saw to that. The ungodly impulses of this spirit-receiver are responsible for man's depravity. This is why God gives us a NEW Spirit, the Spirit of Christ. This new Spirit is turned to one station only—G-O-D. The point? Everything about a man, except his body, IS SPIRIT. So don't be confused when we sometimes speak of man's soul as the spiritual image of God. We are NOT referring to his spirit when we say that.

THE CHARACTERISTICS OF THE TWO NATURES

The old nature, (old man), which exists alongside the new, remains just as he was before salvation. He is "corrupt according to deceitful lusts" (Eph. 4:22), and is "born of the flesh" (John 3:6). Nothing changes within the old nature, and because he is dominated by Satan he can

86

exhibit only the works of the flesh. These are described in detail in the fifth chapter of Galatians:

> Now the works of the flesh are manifest which are these; adultery, fornication, uncleanness, lasciviousness, idolatry, witchcraft, hatred, variance, emulations, wrath, strife, seditions, heresies, envyings, murders, drunkenness, revilings and such like; of the which I tell you before, as I have also told you in the past, that they which do such things shall not inherit the kingdom of God (vss. 19-21).

Whenever these things are found in anyone's life you can be sure the nature controlling him is not the new one. It is the old man who does these things, and it is he that is excluded from heaven. All Christians can find some of these things in their own lives; things which are definite marks of depravity and clear evidences of the old man's active survival. One can praise God that the old man "shall not inherit the kingdom of God:" only the **new.** (Gal. 5:21)

The old man cannot do otherwise. He remains bound to the "prince of the power of the air, the spirit that now worketh in the children of disobedience" in a continuing slavish bondage. He is the child of the devil, and as such, can do no righteousness. He can only sin.

The new man is a new creation. God does not take the old nature and make it over. As far as He is concerned it is dead and "passed away." It is the new man that God is interested in. This is the person who is going to spend eternity with Him. This new man is ". . . created in righteousness and true holiness" (Eph. 4:24). He cannot sin. He has a perfect, sinless nature — a nature which can manifest only the "fruit of the Spirit" i.e., "love, joy, peace, longsuffering, gentleness, goodness, faith, meekness, temperance . . ." (Gal. 5:22-23). This nature is as perfect as Christ for it is His very own.

What a spot for man to be in! He stands between two diametrically-opposed natures—between one which cannot sin and one which can only sin. The two natures are as different as night and day. Possessed of two warring spirits, each seeking to manifest his respective attributes, the believer is faced with deciding which shall control him. The free soul, the image of God, may choose whichever he wishes. The one he chooses will control him for as long as he allows it. What a place of sovereignty! The child of God can now direct a great host of spiritual power. The power of God and the power of Satan stand poised. They await only the signal of the believer's free will.

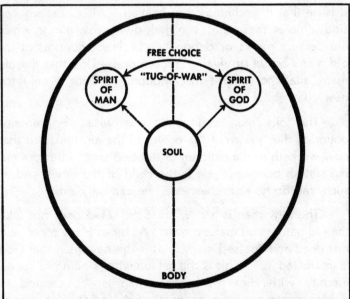

Here the soul of the believer is shown between the two opposing spirits. He is still free to choose between them, but the one he chooses, whether God or Satan (self), will be the one he will entertain in his thinking and exhibit in his behavior. There is no way to serve both at the same time. Even if the surrender lasts for only seconds, it has to be to one or the other.

It is important for us to remember that God never interferes with man's freedom of choice —either before salvation or after. The **Christian** is as free to surrender to the "spirit of man" as he is to the "Spirit of Christ." He will always be surrendered to one or the other. Paul reminds the Romans of this choice. "Know ye not that to whom ye yield yourselves servants to obey, **his** servants ye are to whom ye obey; whether of sin unto death, or of obedience unto righteousness?" (Rom. 6:16). Surrender to the old man can only produce sin which is the cause of death. Surrender to the new man yields an obedience which results in righteousness.

Paul recognized this control of the two spirits over his own soul. When he was surrendered to the "Spirit of Christ" and manifesting the fruit of that surrender, he testified, "Not I, but Christ that dwelleth in me." He was aware that any goodness coming from him was the "by-product" of Christ's indwelling presence. When he was surrendered to the "spirit of man" and manifesting the fruit of that surrender, he would exclaim, "It is no more I that do it, but sin that dwelleth in me" (Rom. 7:17). His sinful acts and the evil coming from him were "by-products" of the indwelling "spirit of disobedience." Paul, as the seventh chapter of Romans teaches, knew well that his life was dominated by spiritual forces. The contest between them was fought on the battlefield of his soul.

How thrilling it is to contemplate that we can, by surrender to the indwelling Holy Spirit, actually manifest the blessedness of our Lord Jesus. Our joy, peace and sweetness are directly proportional to the degree of our surrender to Him. When we are gentle to others and seek to do things that bring joy and blessing to their lives, we can be sure that the Lord, Himself, is motivating our words and deeds. When we are unkind to our wives and lose our tempers with the children, we can be sure that our surrender is not to Him. Our homes provide a wonderful place to learn lessons of surrender and to measure our true spirituality. This is one of the hardest places to let Jesus have the control of our lives. Surrender to Him in the midst of the marriage situation can produce an abundance of Christ-like fruit.

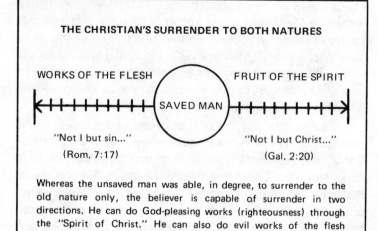

THE CHRISTIAN'S SURRENDER TO BOTH NATURES

WORKS OF THE FLESH

FRUIT OF THE SPIRIT

SAVED MAN

"Not I but sin..."
(Rom. 7:17)

"Not I but Christ..."
(Gal. 2:20)

Whereas the unsaved man was able, in degree, to surrender to the old nature only, the believer is capable of surrender in two directions. He can do God-pleasing works (righteousness) through the "Spirit of Christ." He can also do evil works of the flesh through the "spirit of disobedience." The degree to which he surrenders to either spirit, is the degree he will manifest either of his two natures.

It is easy to forget that the Sovereign Christ dwells in our hearts. Even when we study the doctrine of His precious indwelling, just as we are now, it is not easy to appropriate the full truth of it. It is just so many words rather than an experience. Many Christians are miserable because of this. They have Christ, to be sure, but they know nothing of the blessedness that could be theirs if only He had control. These same ones will go to church and sing, "If you want joy, joy, joy, let Jesus come into your heart." Yet for all their singing they are unhappy, because He doesn't really dominate them. They have Him; but He doesn't have them. Their surrender is still mainly directed toward the old man. Their lives reflect Satan's domination rather than Christ's. They are very restless.

heaven   world

Perhaps the song title should be changed; better it should read, "If you want misery, let Jesus come into your heart and then ignore Him." Such a policy brings just that. The Christian who has received Christ and yet finds the things of his former life more attractive, has misery. How striking are Jesus' own words at this very point, "No man can serve two masters. . ." To attempt to live with "one foot in the world and the other in heaven" is to invite bitter distress.

The Galatians were taught to think of the struggle between the two natures as a "tug-o-war." "For the flesh lusteth against the Spirit, and the Spirit against the flesh; and these are **contrary** the one to the other: so that ye **cannot** do the things that ye would" (Gal. 5:17). The two spirits vie with each other for mastery of the believer. The Spirit of Christ and the spirit of man both plead for control of the Christian's life and contend for his affections. The believer is free to choose which it shall be. This is a freedom that God has determined not to violate, and one for which the Christian must give account — he is fully responsible for his choice.

THE NATURE OF CHRISTIAN GROWTH

The new man that comes into being upon the instant of salvation is but an infant. The little new creation may be likened to a naturally born child who has just entered the world. He is feeble, needing care and time before he can gain strength. The Apostle Peter says he is a "new-born babe" and as such should "desire the sincere milk of the Word" that he might grow. God expects the new man to grow. In fact, the writer to the Hebrews is almost hostile when discussing this. He finds some are still babes; requiring milk when they ought to be teachers and partaking of strong meat. He is distressed with their immaturity and rebukes his readers for their failure to grow (Heb. 5:12-14).

The care of the newly-born, spiritual infant is similar to that of the naturally born child. First of all, one looks for **breath** in the new arrival. When a baby makes his first appearance, the doctor often gives him a pat on the "backside" to make him cry. He does this to make sure that breathing has started. A baby has to breathe. He wouldn't last long if he didn't. **Prayer** is "breath" to the new Christian. This is developed first in the newly-won convert.

The next thing a baby needs is milk or **food**. He can go longer without food than he can without breath, but he needs food right away if he is to grow. To survive, the natural child must have his bottle. The "Bread of Life" or the **Word of God**, is "food" to the Christian. He needs this soon if normal growth is to follow. This is Bible study coming to him in one of its many forms.

The tiny little fellow needs something else, if he is to develop. He needs **exercise.** Brand new muscles are essentially powerless, but with exercise they gain strength rapidly. The child in his crib sends his arms in every direction in wild, uncontrolled movements, but they supply needed exercise. **Service** is the "exercise" the new Christian must have. He needs to get active right away. No doubt he will be content just to be with the other members of the family for awhile, as he adjusts himself to the new surroundings, but before long he should get busy with some activity of his own.

Thus it is the new "babe in Christ" has three early needs for his growth; prayer, Bible study, and some form of service. Growth is important. God does not take us out of the world the moment we make our decision to receive Jesus. He leaves us here — not just because there are jobs He wants us to do, but because life here on earth can produce growth in the spiritual man. Just as the physical or natural man, the product of the first birth, needs time to grow; so also does the spiritual man. God does not want undeveloped persons in heaven. The earth is the ideal place for both men to grow.

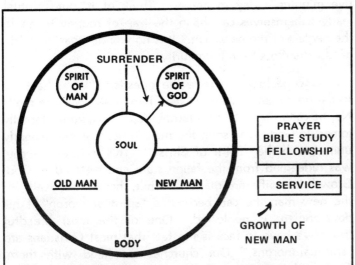

For as long as the believer is surrendered to the indwelling Spirit of God, he exhibits the "new man" only. He will manifest this new nature in so far as it has developed. If he is but a babe in Christ, he will display but little maturity. If he has worked hard to be like Christ, he could display considerable maturity. The growth of the soul (person) is the name of the game as far as God is concerned.

A Christian does not have to feed or develop the new man if he does not wish to. Here again he is free to do as he pleases. He may, if he chooses, delight himself in the things that nurture the old man instead. He can spend most of his life manifesting the old nature and exhibiting the old man if that is his preference. It's a tragedy when this happens, but unfortunately it is very common. Many Christians do not care to build up their new man at all. When this is the case, it is a terrible waste of one's life.

One wonders just what is the actual development of most Christians. The average believer spends almost no time in the Word. He's so busy making a living and caring for worldly responsibilities, that only a fraction of his time is devoted to things of the Spirit. It is reliably estimated that the average preacher spends but five minutes a day in prayer. Think of it, our spiritual leaders themselves caught in the trap of routine living to the neglect of the new man. It is no wonder that the body of Christ suffers from immaturity.

One could justly raise the question, "What happens to the new man if we don't feed him at all. Will he die?" No, he can't die. He has eternal life; that is, he is eternally joined to God. The soul, the man himself, is permanently united with the "Spirit of Christ." This is how the soul was redeemed from the fallen state and restored to God. Growth is a different matter. While there is no death for the new man, he can become a "spiritual moron" if his development is neglected. One of the most dreadful truths we have to face is the fact that most Christians are "spiritual morons." Our churches are filled with them. Their pitiful condition must surely tear at the heart of God. These are His own dear ones whom He has redeemed for Himself. They spend ten, twenty, thirty; yea, even fifty years with almost imperceptible growth. They take a little "milk" now and then when they should have long since partaken of the strong meat of God's word. Most pastors find their hands tied as a result of such Christians. They can't preach the deeper truths. Their audiences are in no condition to receive them. The family of God suffers serious deficiency when we permit this. I trust, dear reader, this has not been the story of your life.

THERE IS A DIFFERENCE
BETWEEN SURRENDER AND GROWTH

We ought not to confuse these two concepts of Christian living. They are not the same. The surrender of the brand new Christian is the **same** as the surrender of the developed Christian. The difference between them is not in the degree of their surrender but in what they have to surrender. The mature saint has **more** to surrender to God, but the act itself is no different from that of the babe. The mature Christian has more knowledge, skill and understanding and in his surrender he presents these to the Lord. Yet, doing so differs none from the babe who gives his bit to the Lord.

The more we grow the greater is our **capacity** for service. That's the importance of growth. It increases our capacity for service and revealing Christ to others. Growth in the Christian is much like sharpening an axe. The same stroke (surrender) cuts much more wood. One can say, "Lord, I give myself to Thee," but if he's trained and equipped as a soul-winner and soul-builder, he can do more for Christ. The surrender that he makes, however, is the same as that of the newer babe.

A Note on Growth

There are some thoughts on growth that should be a part of your understanding.

Man does not grow like a vegetable. Because he has a free will, he may not grow at all. A head of lettuce cannot decide to resist growth and maturity, but a man can. He can, by his own choice, remain immature.

Growth, as God desires it, is always in His own like-ness. For the Christian, growth means maturing in the likeness of Jesus; in His patience, forgiveness, long suffer-ing, and so on. These are things which cannot be learned simply by reading of them in a book — even the Sacred Book. They can be learned only in actual experiences. That is, one must suffer a long time if he is to become long-suffer-ing. He must be in a nerve racking situation that demands patience before he can begin to cultivate it for himself. If he is to learn self-control, then he must be in situations that would cause him to "blow his top," as the expression goes. Otherwise, his learning is all in his head and not in his life.

What we are saying is that God produces the kind of growth He wants by sending stressful circumstances into our lives. He uses sickness, suffering, tragedy, disappoint-ments, to name but a few, in accomplishing maturity within His children. God never touches our wills. He simply manipulates the external circumstances so that our wills must operate under the pressure of distressing situations. It's up to us whether we hate or forgive; whether we become anxious or rest in faith. He sends the circum-stances — we provide the response.

Man would have the opposite. He feels that the best in life is achieved when there's money in his pocket and he can spend leisure in good health. He doesn't know that comforts and ease rot the human. History has proved this so often. If man does not grow, he regresses. He cannot stand still; life always moves. The things that men desire from life lead to regression. The things that God sends lead to maturity.

Another thing important here is the matter of our reward. If our growth enables us to have larger and more effective ministries, we can expect greater reward at the hand of our Master. It is one of His great delights to honor and reward His children. He can't do it, though, if they have not earned them or deserve them. It is interesting that the roll call of heroes in the eleventh chapter of

Hebrews consists of those who looked forward to the reward of God. Moses is honored because "...he was looking to the reward" (Heb. 11:26).

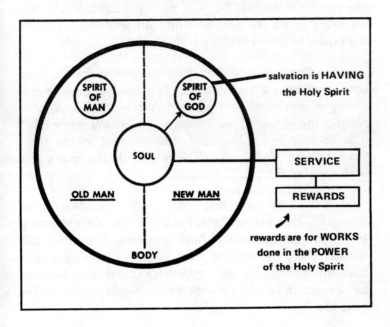

NOTE THAT REWARDS HAVE TO DO WITH THE SOUL.

Even though a soul is surrendered to the Spirit, it is the PERSON who actually does the reward-bearing deeds. Rewards are not earned by the Holy Spirit for the believer, neither are they given for HAVING the Holy Spirit. They are bestowed on the Christian for what HE has done. Having the Spirit makes it possible for one to do works in His power. The soul does the work. The Spirit supplies the power.

This is illustrated by the figure of power brakes, such as are on our automobiles. The driver exerts **his**

pressure against the car's brake pedal, but the engine-produced hydraulic pressure activates the brakes. The driver of the machine actually brakes the car **in the power of** the engine. So it is with the believer. He sets his heart to do the will of God, but actually does it in the power of the indwelling Holy Spirit.

The Christian is rewarded for everything that he does because of his surrender to the Holy Spirit — even to the giving of a "cup of cold water." When Jesus says, concerning the doing of such things, "... in My name ...," it is as though He had said, "surrendered to the Holy Spirit." (Matt. 10:42) We determine to **do** the works and God supplies the power **for** them.

Perhaps you may ask, "What are the rewards we receive?" "Reward" is a term the Bible uses when referring to the job each of us will have in heaven. This future job is determined by our faithfulness in this life. If we accept the responsibility to use our lives for Christ now, then we can expect to be trusted with greater responsibility in the next life.

THE GLORY THAT AWAITS THE BELIEVER

The Christian has two natures in this life alone. The struggle between them or the "tug-o-war" exists only so long as he is in the body. A wonderful thing happens when physical death occurs. The old man is completely removed and the new man stands alone. He has been developed through the afflictions endured, plus the contest of his natures. But in that day it will all end. Maybe it should be called "Graduation Day," for that is what happens. The believer graduates from the "struggle school" into a new-life adventure with God. One of the first things that

98

thrills the new Christian is the truth of "Absent from the body to be present with the Lord."

Not only does physical death put an end to our time of probation on earth, it also puts an end to our struggle between our two natures. When this body dies, our old nature passes away with it. How come? It lives in the flesh only. When we received Christ, a spiritual surgery took place. That old nature was circumcised off the soul. The apostle Paul refers to it as a circumcision of the heart (Rom. 2:29). It continues to live in the flesh to plague us as long as we are in these bodies. But once the body is put off, the old nature goes with it. All that is left is the soul with its new nature. That is what is ushered into heaven.

Does physical death leave us unclothed? Indeed not. There is a spirit "form" which we wear in the Lord's presence in heaven that is as perfectly suited to life in the spirit as our physical bodies are to life on earth. Our physical bodies are, in fact, nothing more than "earth suits" used to get about in space and time. Once we're out of these bodies, we operate in a spirit form that is eternal and unseen (2 Cor. 4:18). What is that "form" like? We don't know. But it is like the form Jesus has now. Obviously it is some kind of a form which makes no contact with the flesh, for Jesus lives in our hearts right now.

Yet, a day is coming when we will need a NEW PHYSICAL form. We will need it to appear in the resurrection when the Lord returns as promised. He will have a glorified body in that day and so will we. Ours will match His, "for our citizenship is in heaven from whence we look for the Savior, the Lord Jesus Christ: Who shall CHANGE our body of humiliation that it might be fashioned like unto His glorious body. . ." (Phil. 3:20,21).

In that day when He appears, "then shall ye also appear with Him in glory" (Col. 3:4).

In the day of resurrection and our appearing with the Lord, we will still be the SAME persons. Death has no effect on us. We have already seen how the soul has its own independent life. It was designed to survive without a physical body, even as do all who are in hell and heaven. But for the grand appearing of the Lord, and our appearing with Him, we need a GLORIFIED body. This is the one of which Paul speaks in the 15th chapter of 1st Corinthians. The resurrection body will be much like the old body, but it will **not** have a second nature.

The glorified body will be spiritual. I did not say SPIRIT, but spiritual. There's a difference. This will be a physical body subject to spiritual commands. Our old bodies were carnal and we were subject to them. If they got hungry we had to feed them. If they were tired, we put them to bed. But this will not be true of the new body. It will do anything its spiritual owner desires. That's why Paul says, "it is sown a natural body, it is raised a spiritual body." There are two kinds as he is careful to point out, "There is a natural body and there is a spiritual body" (1 Cor. 15:44).

In that glorious day we will reign with our Lord Jesus on the earth. It will be a restored earth as we saw in the first chapter. Yet we will be exactly the same people. Our souls will be as they are right now. In fact, I doubt if we will even notice the transition. We will slip from one phase to another with no change in ourselves. Of course, we will be very much like Jesus, for our old natures will be gone and we will display only the new man. Yet in that day, we will be a whole body, spirit (Christ's) and soul. That's why we pray, "Even so come quickly, Lord Jesus."

100

LOOK AT THE DRAWING

Turn to the completed visual at the end of the chapter. See the three stages of the believer's life—past, present, and future? When we were unsaved, we had but one nature. It is pictured on the left of the drawing. That represents our PAST.

The large circle in the center pictures the PRESENT stage, that of regenerate man. The moment we received the Spirit of Christ, a new nature was immediately created, so that we had two natures side by side. In this stage we grow, manfesting godly changes referred to as the "fruit of the Spirit." We can also do the works of the flesh if we want to, for we are free to obey the call of either nature.

It is the struggle between our two natures that makes Christian development possible. Without this struggle, there is no way to grow in godliness. When a man has a choice, he must deliberately deny himself and put down the desires of the flesh. The spiritual growth of the believer is represented by dotted lines extending the new man side of the soul. There are no such lines on the old man's side. He is NOT to grow. He won't if we put Jesus first and resist the appeals of the flesh. To develop as he ought, the new man must make use of such means as Bible study, prayer, fellowship, and witnessing to the lost.

Now look to the lower right-hand corner. There the glorified man is pictured, our FUTURE state on earth. This is how we will look when we appear with the Lord. When Jesus comes back we will be WITH Him, and we will have a body like His. The body will be PHYSICAL, yet glorified body. Yet we will be the SAME soul joined to the Spirit of Christ. In that future stage we will exhibit the growth we made during the time we had two natures.

We will use the glorified body only so long as Jesus reigns on earth. When it comes time for Him to end the earthly reign and surrender the kingdom back to God the Father, we will no longer use ANY PHYSICAL body (1 Cor. 15:24). From then on, we will use the spirit FORM which is suited to the eternity of heaven.

SUMMARY

We have seen just how the receiving of the Holy Spirit or "Spirit of Christ" makes it possible for the believer to become a whole new man. Human depravity is overcome when we surrender to the indwelling Holy One for His power operates within us to manifest the fruit of the Spirit (or godliness) through us.

The life in the flesh and the struggle of the soul between the two natures provides for the growth and maturity of the Christian. There can be no growth without struggle. The muscle of an arm withers unless it is put to use. The same is true of the unexercised soul. How wise is our God in making provision for this needed stress. Even the circumstances of life are not allowed to remain tranquil for too long. Upheaval and tragedy come to every life sooner or later. God knows there is nothing more deadly to the soul than maintaining the "status quo." As a consequence our lives are filled with times of struggle.

Finally, in God's time, we get rid of the old man, with his fears and terrors, through the experience of death. In that day the struggle of this life comes to an end. The chains that bind men to earth are loosed. Great new lessons and adventures in the realm of omniscience and omnipresence await the "graduates" of the "two-nature" school. Even now we can look forward to the fellowship which God has planned. What human mind is able to comprehend the things that God has in store for those who love Him!

Death for the Christian is NOT the terrorizing thing most people fear. It is actually a thrilling event, one which should be anticipated with great joy. But Christians cannot do that until they learn the mechanics of death and how to prepare themselves for it. After that, they get excited thinking how they might use their death as a witness for Christ. Those interested in learning more about our thrilling graduation from this life, will want to read my book, "Death Made Easy." It sheds a great deal of light on this fascinating subject.

THE TWO NATURES OF THE BELIEVER

MAIN TEACHING (Review and Remember)

1. Man is a tripartite being.

2. By means of **pre-salvation illumination** he is enabled to make a decision to receive Christ.

3. Upon his decision he receives the Holy Spirit.

4. This gives him two natures (depraved and holy).

5. He is free to serve one or the other.

6. He is always yielded to one or the other.

7. The "old" man can only sin (works of the flesh).

8. The "new" man cannot sin (fruit of the Spirit).

9. Whichever spirit he surrenders to, will be the man he will reveal.

10. The new man is but a "babe" and needs to grow. As he grows he reveals more and more of the personality of the indwelling Christ when he surrenders to the Holy Spirit.

11. He needs to breathe (prayer). He needs to eat (Bible study). He needs to exercise (service and fellowship).

12. Growth however is not surrender. The more the new man grows the more there is to surrender. The more one has to surrender (by growing) the more he can be used.

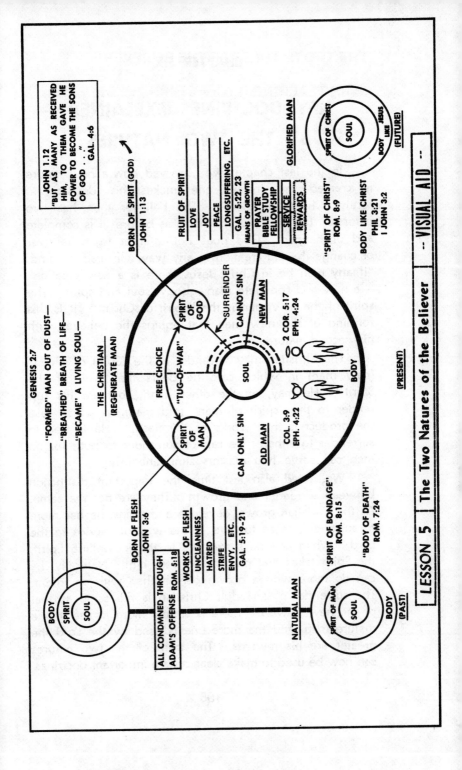

GENESIS 2:7

"FORMED" MAN OUT OF DUST—
"BREATHED" BREATH OF LIFE—
"BECAME" A LIVING SOUL—

JOHN 1:12
"BUT AS MANY AS RECEIVED
HIM, TO THEM GAVE HE
POWER TO BECOME THE SONS
OF GOD . . ." GAL. 4:6

BORN OF SPIRIT (GOD)
JOHN 1:13

THE CHRISTIAN
(REGENERATE MAN)

FRUIT OF SPIRIT
LOVE
JOY
PEACE
LONGSUFFERING, ETC.
GAL. 5:22, 23
MEANS OF GROWTH
PRAYER
BIBLE STUDY
FELLOWSHIP
SERVICE
REWARDS

FREE CHOICE

SPIRIT OF GOD

SURRENDER

CANNOT SIN

NEW MAN

2 COR. 5:17
EPH. 4:24

"TUG-OF-WAR"

SOUL

SPIRIT OF MAN

CAN ONLY SIN

OLD MAN

COL. 3:9
EPH. 4:22

BODY

BORN OF FLESH
JOHN 3:6

WORKS OF FLESH
UNCLEANNESS
HATRED
STRIFE
ENVY, ETC.
GAL. 5:19-21

"SPIRIT OF BONDAGE"
ROM. 8:15

"BODY OF DEATH"
ROM. 7:24

ALL CONDMNED THROUGH
ADAM'S OFFENSE ROM. 5:18

(PRESENT)

GLORIFIED MAN

SPIRIT OF CHRIST
SOUL
BODY LIKE JESUS

"SPIRIT OF CHRIST"
ROM. 8:9

BODY LIKE CHRIST
PHIL 3:21
1 JOHN 3:2

(FUTURE)

NATURAL MAN

SPIRIT OF MAN
SOUL
BODY

(PAST)

LESSON 5 | The Two Natures of the Believer | -- VISUAL AID --

CHAPTER SIX

KEY DOCTRINES EXPLAINED
BY THE TWO NATURES

In the last chapter we observed how a new nature is created the instant one makes his decision to receive Christ as Saviour. The believer then has two natures. The old nature remains as before; it is complete and unchanged. God does not attempt to make over or change the old creation in any way. Instead we find, "If any man be in Christ Jesus there is a new creation" — a new and complete man — body, soul and spirit. The spirit of the new man is the "Spirit of Christ." It is this forming of the new man that eqips the believer with his second nature.

The Christian may surrender to the "Spirit of Christ" (new man) in which case he bears the "fruit of the Spirit." He may, on the other hand, continue his surrender to the "spirit of man" (old man), in which case the product is the "works of the flesh." He is free to surrender to either. He cannot surrender to both for no man can serve two masters simultaneously.

We noted also last time the important distinction between surrender and growth. They are not the same. As the Christian grows, develops and trains, he has more to surrender; more to give in the way of service to the Lord. When anyone surrenders to the indwelling Spirit, the Spirit takes that person and uses him. Naturally, he can do more with a grown person than with an infant. The surrender of an adult Christian is the same as that of the new convert. There is simply more to use in the mature man, and the more one is used by the Lord the greater are his rewards. The truth of the two natures can now be used to make clear certain important doctrines.

THE SECURITY OF THE BELIEVER

The believer is secured by Christ. A glance at the visual aid shows salvation pictured as **having** the "Spirit of Christ." A man must have the "Spirit of Christ" in order to be saved. "Now if any man have not the Spirit of Christ," says the Scripture, "he is none of His" (Rom. 8:9b). The words of the beloved Apostle John reinforce this truth, "Hereby we know that He (Christ) abideth in us by the Spirit which he has given us" (I John 3:24b). With his decision for Christ, one receives the Spirit of God. Having Him, he has eternal life. The life is described as eternal, not because God hands man a "chunk" of life labeled "eternal life," but because men receive the person of Christ Himself. Christians have God dwelling within them. Eternal life, as we have studied in a previous lesson, is not the adding of some life substance to one's soul, but **union** with God.

The Christian possesses the Holy Spirit **completely** in the instant of salvation. One either has Him or he doesn't. He is a **Person**. It is not possible to have only a part of a person. However, the Spirit's **complete possession** of the believer is another matter. This comes about through a total surrender and is accompanied by dramatic changes.

Note: Those who emphasize the phenomena which may follow the Spirit's complete possession of the Christian, generally refer to it as "the baptism." But this "baptism" ought not be confused with the baptism of the believer into "The Body of Christ," which takes place the moment one is saved. Those wishing to teach "the baptism" doctrine, need but make the distinction between the **two complete possessions** in order to use this lesson.

Before Jesus went to the cross He counseled His disciples regarding the Spirit's coming. He referred to Him as the "Comforter." "When the Comforter is come," He said, "He will abide with you forever" (John 14:16). This Person was to abide with them forever and comfort them. Yet, while it is true that He does come and brings the greatest comfort, His very presence within men guarantees more than comfort. It guarantees something else.

In chapter five of Second Corinthians Paul unfolds a startling consequence of the Spirit's indwelling. First, he notes that upon the moment of physical death the Christian appears immediately in the presence of Christ clothed with an eternal form. Then, he supports his statement with a wonderful observation, "He who has prepared us for this very thing is God, who has given us the Spirit as a **guarantee**" (2 Cor. 5:5 RSV). The guarantee, notice, is to the Christian. God has given us the Holy Spirit as a guarantee that we will stand before Him when physical death comes. Having the Holy Spirit we are **personally** guaranteed to "be absent from the body and to be present with the Lord." The Third Person of the Godhead is, Himself, the guarantee of our presence in heaven.

Let's suppose, by way of illustration, that you are the fourth member of a yachting party. You are invited to travel aboard the yacht with a man and his wife and small son. As the boat nears the middle of the harbor, suddenly there's an explosion. The craft begins to sink. The power dingy, which holds but three people, is broken out and the man, his wife and son all get in. He calls to you and promises to return and take you off the sinking yacht. Wouldn't there be some misgiving in your heart? All manner of thoughts would go through your mind, "Perhaps he won't even try to come back for me."

But suppose you hear the man say, "Here son, you hop out and I'll come back for you and our friend." Then

108

the man says to you, "I'll leave my son there with you and when I have left my wife safe on the shore I'll come back for you both." A sigh of relief would no doubt come to your lips. You can breathe easier now for you know the man will return. No need to worry. He has left his son as a guarantee that he will return. Yes, he'll come back: he'll keep his promise.

Our salvation is much like that. We are left in a sinking world that is headed toward terrible destruction with every tick of the clock. But there are those Christians on board whom God has promised that they should not perish. He guarantees that the fate of the world shall not be theirs: that they will be with Him forever. His statement to the point is that they "should not perish, but have everlasting life." He guarantees it and the guarantee is a Person: the third member of the Godhead.

For the believer to go to hell the Father and the Son would have to repudiate and abandon the Holy Spirit. They would have to turn their back upon Him. If the Christian were ever to become lost the Holy Spirit would have to be lost also, for He has come to "abide forever." But praise God such a thing is impossible. The believer is as secure as the Father, Son and Holy Spirit are ONE.

In coming to abide with us forever, the person of the Holy Spirit is sometimes placed in a very uncomfortable position. It is not something we care much to think about, but the Comforter can be made very uncomfortable by having to put up with the things that Christians do and think. Paul knows this and is actually begging us not to hurt Him when he says, "Grieve not the Holy Spirit of God whereby ye are sealed until the day of redemption" (Eph. 4:30). He cannot leave, for His ministry is to seal — sealing us for God and keeping us secure until the day of our delivery.

The Christian is actually a possession of the Lord. He is bought and paid for in full by Christ's work in his behalf. The fact that the believer is left in the world

109

after he has received Christ does not mean that he is any less the Lord's property. He still belongs to God even though he remains in the world and has two contrasting natures. Having bought this possession (the believer), at the "price of His own blood," God seals it for Himself until He is ready to take delivery. The sealing guarantees the delivery. Thus the Christian is signed (purchased), sealed and ready to be delivered: God's purchased possession in the world.

Paul seemingly exhausts himself in attempting to describe the security of God's own. He lists one thing after another which cannot "separate us from the love of God" including life and death (Rom. 8:38,39). He further certifies the absolute character of our security when he observes that God will bring to completion all the work that He has begun in us "in the day of Jesus Christ" (Phil. 1:6). God will see to it that the salvation process, which begins with our "yes" decision, ends with successful completion. Even as a railroad boxcar is sealed for delivery to the customer, the Christian's salvation cannot be disturbed.

Paul has a wonderful verse in Ephesians that sums up very nicely all we've just said:

> In whom ye also trusted, after that ye heard the word of truth, the Gospel of your salvation: in whom also after that ye believed, ye were sealed with that Holy Spirit of promise, which is the earnest (guarantee) of our inheritance until the redemption (taking away) of the purchased possession unto the praise of his glory (Eph. 1:113,14).

"In whom ye were sealed," says Paul, sealed by the Holy Spirit who is the personal guarantee of our inheritance until Christ comes to take His purchased possession. We are already purchased by Christ's blood; sealed by the third member of the Godhead with our future delivery unto God guaranteed. How wonderful it is to have this guarantee. We are in the world, but we belong to God. There's not one thing that Satan can do to thwart our future delivery. We even have the witness within ourselves; "The Spirit itself (Himself) beareth witness with our spirit that we are the children of God." How glorious to be saved and know it!

SALVATION AND REWARDS

The moment we receive Christ we become the "sons of God." This is the content of some precious verses; "But as many as received him to them gave he power to become the sons of God" (John 1:12); "For as many as are led by the Spirit of God, they are the sons of God" (Rom. 8:14); "Beloved now are we the sons of God . . ." (I John 3:2). We become the sons of God upon receipt of the Holy Spirit; and because He has come to abide forever, we remain the Sons of God forever. Our sonship is eternal.

Thus all Christians sojourn in the world divinely labeled as the sons of God. They continue to enjoy and endure the experiences of earthly life as before, but now equipped with two natures instead of one. The world suddenly becomes different to them: it takes on a new character and meaning. The Christian pilgrimage becomes the "challenge of choice." The acquisition of a second nature instantly thrusts the believer into the "valley of decision" for now his new Christian walk consists of choosing between his two natures. This, of course, is God's ingenious plan for bringing His sons to maturity.

The believer is absolutely free to choose between his natures. The will of man is never touched at all. Surrender to the "spirit of man" means that Satan will dominate the life and the works of the flesh will be exhibited as long as the surrender continues. If the surrender is made to the "Spirit of Christ," then it is Christ that uses the Christian to manifest the fruit of the Spirit.

A glance at the visual reveals the child of God squarely in the center of this God-purposed struggle.

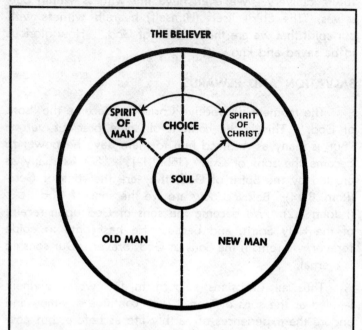

See how the SOUL (person) is FREE to choose between his two natures. If he elects to submit to the "spirit of man," that spirit will prod him to do the works of the flesh. If he yields to the "Spirit of God," that Spirit will prompt him to bear the fruit of the Spirit. The believer matures as he yields more and more to God's Spirit and less and less to the human spirit. Also note that it is the MAN himself who DOES these things, not the spirit prodding him.

Surrender to either of the indwelling spirits determines the work that will be done in the body. This is the chief point of what we are saying. Surrender determines what we do. The emphasis is on the "DO": the resulting works of surrender. The things that are displayed in the life appear as the **result** of surrender to either of the two natures. It is urgent to see however, that these things are what we DO. These are our works, but they must not be confused with WHO WE ARE. Who we are and what we do are two entirely different subjects. They must not be entangled; they must be seen separately.

To confuse **who we are** with **what we do** is to confound our **persons** with our **works.** These are subjects that require separate treatment if we are to understand the Word of God aright. We are the sons of God because we have the Spirit of Christ. What we DO, as the sons of God, is determined by our surrender to either of our two natures. One is **surrender:** the other **possession.** Possessing the Holy Spirit makes us sons (that's who we **are**): surrender to either spirit produces our works (that's what we **do**).

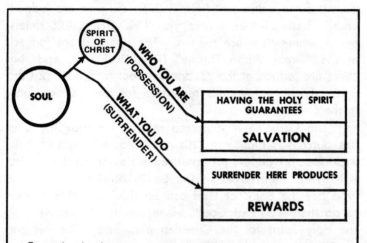

From the drawing you can see the difference between HAVING God's Spirit and the soul's SURRENDER to Him. When the arrow (representing the person's will) is turned to the Spirit, then the soul is submitting to God in some degree. While the believer has ALL of the Spirit, the Spirit does not get ALL of the Christian. Yet, to the degree the Christian yields himself, to that same degree will the Spirit use him for Christ. In the judgment he will be rewarded for everything he has done through surrender to God's Spirit. It is HAVING God's Spirit that makes him a child of God. It is surrender that makes him a good one.

Now we are ready to see the distinction between salvation and rewards. Salvation makes us the sons of God. That's who we are. Rewards are given for our works: what we **do** after we become the sons of God. When these two important truths are mingled Christians suffer confusion. They find unchristian things in their lives and are then tempted to feel their salvation is somehow endangered. This cannot be so as we shall see further on.

There is a judgment for each man's life. Both the saved and unsaved alike must give account to God for their stewardship during the time of their earthly probation. Recall how in chapter two we learned, ". . . It is appointed unto man once to die, but after this the judgment" (Heb. 9:27). All men are judged on the basis of their works, but WHO THEY ARE determines **where** they are judged. The unsaved are judged at the "Great White Throne" (Rev. 20:11-15), and the saints are judged at the "Judgment Seat of Christ" (2 Cor. 5:10). Thus all men are rewarded for their works done in the flesh.

The Christian is expected to live for the One who has purchased him with "His own blood." In fact it is a glorious privilege with great reward awaiting those who will invest themselves in the Lord's service. Only one who has the Spirit of God can do this. It takes power to do the "works of God." One needs the power of the Holy Spirit for the Christian ministries. The servant of Christ may be likened to a man operating the "power brakes" on his car. The driver exerts **his pressure,** but the car is slowed in the **power of the engine-supplied pressure.** So it is with the man of God. He sets his heart to serve, but performs his ministry in the power of God. What a tragedy it is when men willingly throw away the opportunity of this life. How true is the expression, "Only one life 'twill soon be past, only what's done for Christ will last."

By virtue of their free choice, Christians can live their lives as they please, but oh, the loss suffered when they live for themselves. Some will be rich in heaven: others will be paupers. They harvest their own sowing. It is a disaster when the stewardship of a Christian life is squandered: when a life redeemed by Christ is spent pursuing the phantom of temporal pleasure. What a sad day it will be for that soul when his judgment appointment arrives. Yet even out of such frightening truth looms the encouraging fact that the Judge of our works is also the Saviour of our persons. Remember, who we are (sons) is what gets us to heaven. What we **do** (works) here on earth determines our job after we get there.

THE MATTER OF SIN IN THE BELIEVER'S LIFE

Having the two natures is an exclusive feature of the Christian. In fact, we can say it is because he has two natures that he is a Christian. His maturity in Christ is made possible by the struggle that the possession of two natures brings. Having to choose between right and wrong is an exercise of the soul. Choosing to please Christ instead of self, when various situations arise, is a part of the developmental process that God has designed for His sons.

Thus we can see how false it is to suggest that we suddenly **stop yielding** to the old nature the moment we are saved. We are continually having to choose between them and our own experiences prove to us that too often we elect to please the old man rather than the new. We all find things that belong to the old nature present within our lives. We don't like to discover them, but they are there nonetheless. What Christian does not find himself angry at times, or jealous. What Christian has not entertained malicious thoughts and even unclean ones. This could never happen were he continually surrendered to the new man.

115

Let's think for a moment what it would actually mean were we never to surrender for a single second to the old man. Never again would we sin. We'd be as holy as God in all of our thinking and acting. It would mean too, that we would fully and completely reveal the Lord Jesus. Surrender to the Spirit of Christ continually would bring from us an actual manifestation of God in the midst of our friends. His own nature would be shed about wherever we walked. Our friends and associates would see a complete and accurate revelation of Christ without fault or blemish of any kind. It is obvious that none can make such a claim as that: Paul couldn't.

Paul, near the end of his ministry, described himself to Timothy as "chief of sinners" (I Tim. 1:15). From prison he wrote, "Not as though I had already attained, either were already perfect . . . I count myself not to have apprehended . . ." (Phil. 3:12,13). He says, and we paraphrase his words, "I don't claim to have arrived. I know that I haven't. But instead, I am willing to forget that mountain of sin behind me and press on to the prize of the high call in Christ. I want to be more like Jesus tomorrow than I am today." That's what Paul communicated to his friends in the final days of his life of service. No one but Jesus could say, "I do **always** those things that please my father" (John 8:29). There's not one of us who can truthfully make such a claim as that, is there? Most everyone will admit that he backslides. But how is that possible if there's never any surrender to the old nature?

Some groups of sincere Christians have laid emphasis upon certain verses of the Word of God to the neglect of others. Some, through ignorance of the two natures, have taught a "holiness" doctrine of sinless perfection. They teach that a man, once saved, can never sin again: that he is spotless and sin is an impossibility. These people are not to be condemned. Instead, they are to be congratulated for their dogged faith in God's Word even though their own lives offer seeming contradiction.

Zeal, however, apart from knowledge ususally produces confusion and contradiction in even the most devoted disciples of our Lord. To those suffering under this doctrinal discrepancy, the teaching of the two natures can bring blessed comfort and relief. Many must feel the Spirit's conviction of sin in their lives. That is His job.

The "holiness" teaching has its foundation in a golden text, "Whosoever is born of God doth not commit sin: for his seed (God's seed, Christ) remaineth in him: and he cannot sin because he is born of God" (I John 3:9). Many a Christian has read this verse and wondered about it. He reasons, "Why, I'm born of God. How does this apply to me? I know that I sin." The wonderment is easily understood. We know we sin daily, yet here is an explicit statement, "Whosoever is born of God doth not commit sin." How shall we understand this?

When it says, "Whosoever is born of God," this can only refer to the new man; only he is born of God. The old man is "born of the flesh;" not of God. That old man or old nature was acquired by our first birth. Hence the verse is not saying that the Christian doesn't sin. It is saying that the **new man** doesn't sin: that he cannot sin. To this we agree.

The verse adds a further clue, "for his seed remaineth in him." The Seed is Christ, and Christ dwells in the new man. It is the Spirit of Christ that makes the new man and is manifested through him. It is because the "Spirit of Christ" cannot sin that this verse is so. Because Christ cannot sin, the new man cannot sin. Here we have evidence that our interpretation is correct. Christ abides in the new man and the new man abides in Christ. We can therefore accept the holiness teaching as it pertains to the new man, but not to the walk of the believer. He has two natures and manifests them both.

117

The first chapter of First John has the same author as the third chapter. In some Bibles, the first chapter and the third may be compared by glancing across the page. Two significant references seem to stand out in bold contrast. John notes in chapter one, "If we say that we have no sin we **deceive ourselves,** and the truth is not in us. . .if we say that we have not sinned, we make him a **liar,** and his word is not in us" (1 John 1:8-10)—a strong indictment of those who profess to have no sin in their lives! On the other hand, the same writer holds that those born of God cannot sin (3:9). What a terrible contradiction would exist were it not for the fact of the believer's two natures. How precious becomes our doctrine now. It beautifully unfolds the truth of God's Word.

When John, in his first chapter, speaks of the Christian's sin, he has reference to the **old nature.** His words might be put this way, "If we say that we never surrender to the old man we certainly are deceiving ourselves. We most surely do." When he says that the one born of God cannot sin, he is obviously referring to the **new nature.** Here he is saying, "When we are surrendered to the new man we cannot sin, for it is Christ that is doing the work through us." How simple this is. What at first appears to be a contradiction is easily understood in the light of the believer's two natures.

Sinless perfection is not found in any life but Jesus'. He alone was sinless and perfect. Sinless perfection belongs to the new nature, because it is inherited from Christ by means of the second birth. What an error it is, though, to teach that we never yield to the old nature. The Christian does sin, but he possesses one nature which is sinless. This is what guarantees him of heaven.

An incident within the Corinthian church serves to illustrate how a man can manifest the sins of the old nature and yet be saved. It is recorded in Paul's letter to that church of a man who "had his father's wife."

118

A member of the church was living in incest. So gross was his sin and so damaging to the name of the church that Paul counseled, "Put that fellow out of the church. Get rid of him for he is ruining the testimony of the Lord."

The Corinthian church did not have a very saintly character to begin with. It was filled with strife and party jealousies. Yet this offender's conduct was so bad that he had to be removed. The specific instruction was, "deliver such an one unto Satan for the destruction of the flesh, that the spirit may be saved in the day of the Lord Jesus" (I Cor. 5:5). Casting the fornicator from the assembly allowed him to go the way of the **flesh,** but he himself was certain of salvation in the day of the Lord, for he was also born of the **Spirit.** The meaning and interpretation of such an occurrence would indeed be confused without a clear understanding of the two natures.

Personal workers have a question they put to the new convert in order to seal to his mind the truth of his newly acquired sonship. They ask, "If your boy were involved in a criminal act that sent him to jail for the rest of his life, would he still be your child?" The response comes quickly, "Oh, yes." They see the truth instantly. Then the worker points out the fact that what one **does** is not to be confounded with **who** one is. Certain acts found in the Christian's life cannot change the fact that he is "born of God."

SUMMARY

The truth of the two natures has been used to make clear the matter of one's security in Christ. This is accomplished by an eternal union of the soul with the Spirit of God. This union makes one a son of God by spiritual birth. Then we observed the important distinction between WHO one is and WHAT he does. Children of God may act like the children of the devil. A good many do. This is not so bewildering however, when we learn

119

that the child of God may manifest either of his two natures. Who one is, that is his sonship in Christ, guarantees him of heaven. What he does, determines his job or reward after he gets there. Many Bible passages, otherwise confusing, become clear when handled in the light of this truth.

Note: Those in the Wesleyan-Arminian tradition will find they can easily present these truths if they show them as taking place **by faith.** That as long as a person is in faith, he enjoys union with Christ. But should he destroy his faith by persistent worldliness or abandonment, he forfeits the blessedness of salvation. The writer is aware of the many verses supporting the Arminian position, though he does not prefer it.

KEY DOCTRINES EXPLAINED BY THE TWO NATURES

MAIN TEACHING (Review and Remember)

1. Eternal security
   a. We have received the Spirit of God (1 Cor. 2:12).
   b. The Holy Spirit has come to abide FOREVER (John 14:16).
   c. We are sealed by the Holy Spirit (Eph. 4:30).
   d. The Spirit is our guarantee of presence with God (2 Cor. 5:5 RSV).

2. Salvation and rewards
   a. When we receive the Spirit of Christ, we become the sons of God (Rom. 8:14).
   b. We distinguish between **who we are** (sons) and **what we do** (works).
   c. The Christian has two natures and can choose between them.
   d. The manifesting of either nature produces different works.
   e. All works are tried at the Judgment Seat of Christ and those pleasing to God bring rewards (1 Cor. 3:14).

3. The believer's sin problem
   a. God gives the Christian two natures to exercise the soul.
   b. Believers do surrender to the old man and the result is sin.
   c. This produces a three-fold problem for many:
      (1) Personal conviction is felt because it is the Spirit's work to convict.
      (2) Certain Christian groups say that Christians cannot sin.
      (3) Some Bible passages **seem** to threaten the sinning believer with hell.

121

d. The problem is solved by the doctrine of the two natures:
   (1) We do surrender to the old man (1 John 1:8-10).
   (2) The new man cannot sin (1 John 3:9).
e. Two practical illustrations of the solution:
   (1) Galatians 5:21 refers to the old man. He cannot enter heaven.
   (2) The man cast from the Corinthian church was still saved (1 Cor. 5:5).

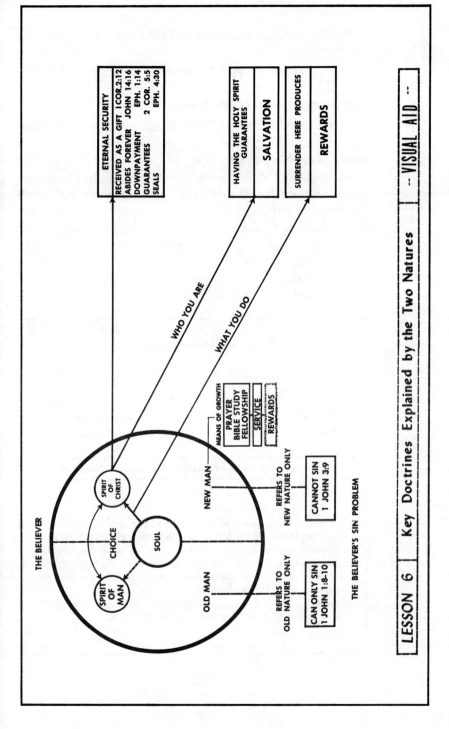

CHAPTER SEVEN

CHRIST THE FIRST CHRISTIAN

THE TWO NATURES OF CHRIST

The cross of Christ often occupies the central place in sermons dealing with Jesus' ministry. Most messages center everything there. We, too, in our lessons so far, when speaking of His work, have laid emphasis on His transition from the flesh to the Spirit via the cross. Yet the entire life of Jesus on earth is every bit as vital to our salvation as the drama of Calvary. The beginning is as significant as the ending. It is the **whole life of Christ**, the incarnation to the transition, that was needed to effect our deliverance from human bondage. This is the truth that will unfold in this chapter.

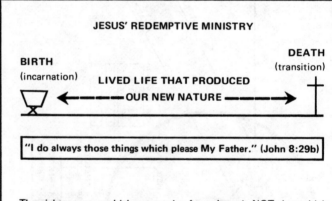

JESUS' REDEMPTIVE MINISTRY

BIRTH
(incarnation)

DEATH
(transition)

LIVED LIFE THAT PRODUCED
◄— — — — — OUR NEW NATURE — — — — —►

"I do always those things which please My Father." (John 8:29b)

The righteousness which we receive from Jesus is NOT that which He owned as the righteous God, but that which He PRODUCED by a life of complete obedience to His Father. It takes this kind of righteousness for men to live with a Holy God. Since Adam was unable to do this, and we are too, it was necessary for Jesus to come and do it for us. Therefore, the Lord not only died on the cross as the sacrifice for our sins, He also lived a holy life which He shares with us by virtue of our living union with Him.

The earthly life of Jesus begins as God appears in human form. Mankind, obviously lost to God through the fall of Adam, could not be recovered and restored to fellowship unless God Himself should come to the rescue. In the appointed time He came. He did not come as a mighty warrior leading an armed host of spiritual soldiers ready to crush the powers that bound man to Satan; He did not come to stand in the midst of the centuries and utter a sin-shattering decree with His lips; He came, rather, to meet Satan on the battle field of moral worth. He came alone. Where the first Adam fell, the "Second Adam" fought the enemy of man's soul. Right there on the same ground. The same contest. The same struggle of the freewill "image of God."

Thus it was that God came as a man. His descent to reach us at the fallen level required great humiliation. This He voluntarily accepted because He loved us so much. Recall, we once said He was willing to do anything to redeem man for Himself. Now we are to learn the extent to which He did go. Paul speaks of God's self-humbling,

> Who, although He existed in the form of God, did not regard equality with God a thing to be grasped, but emptied Himself, taking the form of a bondservant, and being made in the likeness of men. And being found in appearance as man, He humbled Himself by becoming obedient to the point of death, even death on a cross (Phil. 2:6-8 NAS).

What significant words these! Two comparisons stand out. Jesus, we learn, was in the **form** of God and **equal** with God. His form is noted and His equal status. Then we observe the humiliation. He emptied Himself and assumed a **different** form: the form of a servant (man). Thus He was found in the likeness of men, like us.

125

Two things were changed when God came to earth as the Second Adam. His FORM and His RANK (station). His form change was, as we have noted before, from the spiritual to the physical. He now appeared in a body. No longer operating as the **omnipresent God,** He was confined to a single physical body even as we. His rank is lowered infinitely, and this is the real humiliation. He's not a master now, but a servant — a "bondslave" is the Greek meaning of the word. The Babe of Bethlehem's manger stall does not arrive as the Master of the universe, but as a helpless infant. There is one thing that does not change, however, and this point must not be overlooked or missed: there was no change in His **person.** The baby Jesus was exactly the **same** person that He was in heaven. In His being He was God, but the two changes just noted had to occur for God to enter the human stream.

Luke's account of the angel's visit to Mary before our Lord's birth supplies more detail. In verses 26-30 of chapter one, the beloved doctor's gospel records the angel's appearance and pronouncement of divine blessing upon the young virgin. Then follows a bewildering announcement, "And behold thou shalt conceive in thy womb and bring forth a son, and shalt call his name Jesus" (Verse 31). Her marriage to Joseph is not yet consummated and the heavenly messenger informs her that she is to have a child. It is to be a boy and His name is to be Jesus. The poor girl must have been staggered by such news. She has had no contact with any man and yet this stranger tells her, not only that she is to have a baby, but a boy and even his name. We'd be tempted to discredit any doctor that would make such an announcement.

The angel continues, "He shall be great and will be called the **Son** of the Most High (God), and the Lord God will give to him the throne of his **father,** David . . . ." (Verse 32). "You will be the mother, Mary," says the angel, "But God will be His Father." In the same notice her visitor tells that the child is to "sit upon the throne of his father, David." He is to have two fathers; David and God. Obviously, He is not to be sired by two fathers; it couldn't mean that. Rather, He is to be the member of **two families,** simultaneously. He is to be born in the line of Adam (through the house of David) and the line of God.

Poor Mary. How is she to understand all this? She doesn't, so she questions the angel further, "How is this possible seeing I know not a man?" Just bearing a child is beyond her comprehension. While her mind struggles with that mystery the angel speaks an answer, "The Holy Ghost shall come upon thee, and the power of the Highest shall overshadow thee: therefore also that holy thing (Jesus) which shall be born of thee shall be called the Son of God" (Verse 35). "Yes, Mary," says the angel, "you will actually become pregnant by the Holy Spirit; and, by Him, bear a child which shall be called the Son of God."

When we emphasize the fact that Jesus is the Son of God, we sometimes neglect the truth that He was **born** the Son of God. In fact, Jesus was the first person ever to be born of God. Adam is called the son of God, but there the term is used in the creative sense. All men are the sons of God by creation, but something different is meant here. Jesus is the Son of God, not by creation (that's impossible since He's eternal), but by **birth.** This is different. This is why the Scripture refers to Him as the **"first** begotten of the Father." Almost everyone has heard the gospel claim, "God so loved the world that He gave his ONLY BEGOTTEN Son. . ." (John 3:16). His very coming into the world was so that He could be the "first-born among many brethren" (Rom. 8:29b). Others were to come after Him, but at that time He was the only person born of God. The angel heralds the fact that now for the first time in history will one appear who will literally be "born of the Spirit." The blessed Mary was to have the distinct honor of giving birth, not only to David's heir, but the first person ever born of God. Her son was to be twice-born.

Had Jesus been singly born, that is, had He been born of Mary only, His birth would be of the flesh alone. He would still need another birth (born again) and be in the same plight as all natural men. All men born of the flesh, as Jesus once told Nicodemus, need to be born again. "Marvel not," He counselled the Jewish leader, "that I said unto thee, ye must be born again" (John 3:7). Just as men enter the family of Adam by birth, a family in bondage to Satan; so also do men enter the family of God by birth. Birth is the only way in which one can truly be a part of any family. Fleshly birth does not make one a member of the divine family; a second birth is required. That second birth must be spiritual. Naturally there can be no such thing as a second physical birth: it's impossible. There's no such thing as a second spiritual birth either. One of each is all that God had purposed for man.

Luke's verses tell us that Jesus had a double birth. He was born of the Spirit and yet he was also the product of Mary's womb. His appearance was a "twin event." Christ did not have to be born again because He was born of both Mary and the Spirit **at the same time.** Thus it was that He came into the world with two natures.

Now we are to the heart of the matter. It is so vital to see that Jesus entered the world equipped with two natures. This is not a truth that is foreign to Christian orthodoxy. For ages the church has clung to the truth of the two natures of Christ. The councils of the early centuries debated the matter in heated sessions, yet the doctrine withstood all tests. The symbol of the Council of Chalcedon (451 A.D.) has become standard. It certifies that Jesus Christ is one person in His **being** and possessed of two natures. The councils did not attempt to describe **how** the Lord came into possession of two natures, but Christianity has doggedly held to the assertion itself from that time. The discussion that follows will rest within that same framework of doctrinal conviction.

The all important distinction between nature and being must be observed. The truth of Christ is badly clouded when we fail to keep these two elements apart. Jesus is a person: God. He was equipped with two natures. In His **being** He is the Deity: God appearing within space and time. The two natures are His **equipment.** The discovery of this truth unlocks much of the mystery surrounding God in Christ.

Jesus came into the world a saved man. Twice born, and possessed of two natures, our Lord did not need to be delivered from the bondage of Satan. He came as the member of two families, not just one. In this way, His arrival in the world was different from ours. We enter as children born into a single family. We require a subsequent birth in order to attain divine sonship; He did not. Apart from this, however, His coming was no different from that of any other person. He snuggled against His mother as might any other child. He looked no different from any baby. He wasn't either, except for His second nature. He wasn't saved when He was three years old or four, as some are. He was saved from birth.

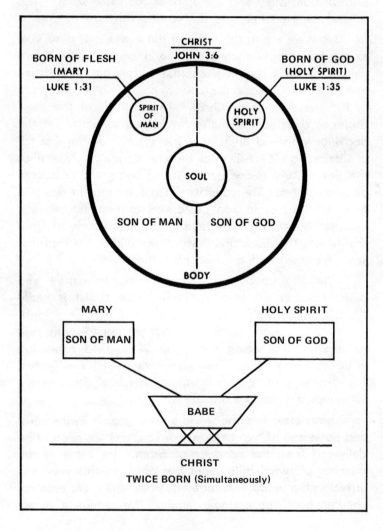

CHRIST
JOHN 3:6

BORN OF FLESH
(MARY)
LUKE 1:31

BORN OF GOD
(HOLY SPIRIT)
LUKE 1:35

SPIRIT OF MAN

HOLY SPIRIT

SOUL

SON OF MAN | SON OF GOD

BODY

MARY

SON OF MAN

HOLY SPIRIT

SON OF GOD

BABE

CHRIST
TWICE BORN (Simultaneously)

130

This of course had to be. If Jesus entered the world with only one nature, then He would have been subject to Satan as the other heirs of Adam. He would have been like the rest of us and would, Himself, need redemption from human bondage. God would have made a terrible mistake had that happened: He would have allowed Himself to become a subject of Satan. He could not then be the Saviour: He would need a Saviour Himself. No, in order for Jesus to be the Saviour, He had to arrive with two natures. Anyway, how could it ever be said that Jesus had to be born again in order to become the Son of God — He **was** God in His person!

When we say that Jesus came into the world a "saved Man," we are referring to His two natures. He was not, of course, a sinner Who had to be rescued from depravity by the acquisition of a second nature. This is true of us, but not of Him. He arrived in the world as a Christian—already equipped with two natures. We want to emphasize that with His two natures, His psychological makeup is identical to that of the born-again Christian. The visual opposite shows Him with His two natures and you can see that He appears no different from any other believer.

A review of the visual that has been employed for the last three lessons shows the saved man with his two natures: "old man" and "new man." The old man is complete with body, soul and spirit. He is the same unchanged, Satan-bound individual that he was before salvation. The new man, created by the receiving of the Spirit of God, is also complete with body, soul and Spirit. This new nature is holy and righteous; giving the believer freedom from sin's domination. The two natures are described by different biblical names: "carnal" and "divine"; "fleshly" and "spiritual." Each is acquired by a separate birth: each reflects membership in a different family.

131

The soul (person) of Jesus is God. (Note this identification on the visual which accompanies this lesson.) God, a person, appearing in human form but in the role of a "saved" man. He is equipped with two natures, as is the Christian, but in His person He is God. Sometimes Jesus is referred to as the God-man, but this is an expression that can be misleading. He is not half-God and half-man, as the term might imply. He is not like the half-man, half-horse creature of Grecian mythology: He is God in His person. God is a person, and clothed in flesh He appears no different from any other person. Paul refers to Him as a man, ". . . the man Christ Jesus" (I Tim. 2:5.) That's just what He is, a man who is God. He is the only One. There is no other man who is God.

Jesus was God come into the world. The baby that was born in Bethlehem was God, but a self-emptied God. This is Paul's expression which further unlocks the mystery of Christ; "But emptied himself, taking the form of a servant . . ." (Phil. 2:7a A.S.V.). Emptied Himself of what? Emptied Himself of everything that makes up the very **majesty** of God. At once it can be seen that God cannot empty Himself of His person: that's a self contradiction. God cannot cease to be God. He cannot empty Himself of His **BEING,** but He can empty Himself of other things. He can, in His humiliation divest Himself of His omnipotence, omniscience and omnipresence. He can and did strip Himself of these things so that He entered the world simply with the pure soul of an infant, an infant with two natures.

Thus it was that Jesus came into this world as did we. He had nothing more within Himself than do we. In His **identity,** which he can never lose, He was God: but an identity of being was all that He had. He "emptied Himself" of all the privileges of majesty. Self-emptied and self-stripped, Christ so dearly loved us that He was willing to relinquish the glory of heaven and the

132

attributes of divinity to save us. Only when we understand the genuine humiliation of Jesus' incarnation can we begin to know the cost of our redemption. The master of the heavens and the universe appeared unto men as the babe of Bethlehem ready to become the "second" Adam. In heaven's glory He enjoyed all that God has and is: in Bethlehem He had nothing — absolutely nothing; no omniscience (all knowledge), no omnipresence (everywhere present), no omnipotence (all power). No longer was He the master of the universe; He was a bondslave and subject to two natures.

THE RESOURCES AND TESTINGS OF CHRIST

The Scripture speaks directly to the point of Christ's humiliation, "Though He was rich, yet for your sakes He became poor, that ye, through His poverty, might become rich" (2 Cor. 8:9). Christ's poverty is a meaningless notion until we become familiar with the extent of His humiliation. He disrobed Himself of all the glory and power that characterizes the Father in heaven. No longer was He a master, but took the role of a "bondslave." In Himself He was powerless and had to grow through the experiences of life. The words of the writer to the Hebrews form a hymn of praise, "Though a Son, yet He learned **obedience** through the things which He suffered" (Heb. 5:8). Think of it, God learning obedience through suffering — as a servant — taking orders! (See Luke 2:52).

It is because of His self-emptying that Jesus testified of His own powerlessness; "Of mine own self I can do nothing." In all of the wonderful things that our Lord performed He never once claimed to have done them in His own power. He did all things in the power of the Holy Spirit which indwelt Him. Always He was careful to state that it was the working of the Father through Him. In His own person He was helpless and powerless, depending completely upon the Father and the Holy Spirit to use Him according to the divine plan. He laid aside everything for us that He might come into the world as do we. This is the way that God chose to come to man in order to rescue him. "I came not to do Mine own will," said Jesus, "but the will of Him that sent Me." From babyhood to manhood and to the cross Jesus took no glory for Himself. He came, not as an all-powerful monarch, but as the Image of God (soul) to tread the same road of human life that is before each of us. He followed the leading of the Spirit in every step that He took: He was led into the wilderness "by the Spirit;" to the Jordan to be baptized by John "in the Spirit;" led from place to place as the Spirit directed; "by the Spirit cast out demons;" all the way to Calvary His life was ordered by the Spirit's direction according to God's master plan. His poverty was complete: He had nothing, not even a place to "lay His head" that you and I might be set free from Satan's grasp.

That God would willingly become a partaker of man's lot is a staggering truth. It is easy to think of Him as the divine Spectator, but now He appears before us as the **central participant.** That evening in Bethlehem, the Creator no longer remained an observer of the human tragedy; now He was found at the very center of it. By virtue of His dual birth, He was ready to enter into and explore fully and completely man's misery and even his death. The angels were truly rocked by the sight they beheld in that manger stall — even a star interrupted its course — for the most spectacular person of all time and eternity was to cry His first breath as might any other child. The Creator humbled and stripped of glory and majesty finding His security in a woman's arms. Only in this way could the infinite One explore finitude. Only in this way could God of very God enter the whirlpool of human existence and "deliver them who through fear of death were all their lifetime subject to bondage" (Heb. 2:15).

GOD!

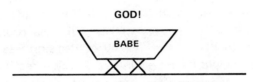

BABE

Heaven was shocked at the sight in the manger stall. A star did strange things. The angels were mystified to see their Creator become a babe. They watched the eternal God lay aside His majesty and might and LIMIT Himself to the capacities of a tiny human body. The baby Jesus was God stripped to His essential being—plus nothing!

What condescension — God, not only emptied, but willing to be equipped with a human nature. We almost shudder when we think that the holy and sinless Christ would allow Himself to come in such close contact with our plight. Yet there was no other way for Him to know **experimentally** the creation's fallen existence. How else could He enter the realm of fallen man? How else could He be **tempted** except sin have the same avenue of access to His soul as it does with ours? (Heb. 2:18).

With His two natures Jesus was in a position to experience everything that comes into the life of any Christian. In fact, He was the first one to live the life of struggle between two natures. Indeed, He was the first one to live the Christian life. It is for this reason that the first chapter of Hebrews claims Him to be the "Pioneer and Perfecter of our faith" (Heb. 12:2). How wonderful; when God asks us to live the Christian life, He is not requesting of us something that He, Himself, has not already done. He has done it — in human form.

Possessed of two natures, one human and the other divine, Christ was able to "be tempted in all points like as we . . . " (Heb. 4:15). By means of the natural and godly natures, He could feel within Himself the pleading of both spirits for mastery of His will. He could know what it is to live in the "valley of decision" as do His saints. He could be tested in every way — feel the same pressures — experience the same internal struggle as do we. He went through the whole of His earthly life facing one decision upon another. Every step of His life called for decision. He was always faced with a choice between His two natures. The Lord could, in this way, know what it is to be tempted in the area of pride. Satan saw to that in the wilderness. Anger was another: the entire list of human sin could be mentioned for there was not one point to which He was not exposed. Worry and worldiness could have easily been found in Him — but they weren't. Yes, it was possible for Him to have yielded to sin, but He didn't. Remember what we said about a perfect man? He is one who **can** sin, but **won't**. This is where our Lord's perfection shines in all its glory.

Think of it — our Lord has faced everything that you and I will ever face without once yielding to it. He refused to yield to the "old man," preferring to please the Father. Even more wonderful to consider is that He had nothing more with which to meet sin's challenge than you and I. His resources were the same as ours. He had no more weapons with which to stand against Satan than we: He couldn't have. How unfair for the Word of God to ask us to "walk even as He walked" if He possessed powers which were beyond ours. He couldn't be our example, could He? We can't follow a man who is equipped with weapons not available to us: we can't emulate one who has such an advantage over us. No, Jesus had nothing more than you and I with which to meet the temptations that were constantly before Him.

"Go away, Satan! For it is written..."
Matt. 4:10

His resources were the same as ours. He met all temptations by the Word and prayer, trusting the Holy Spirit to enable and deliver Him. We have the same. Of course we don't spend whole nights in prayer. He did. He preferred the fellowship of the Father to any of the world. He hungered for moments when He could be alone and quietly enjoy His Father in heaven. It became His passion to do the will of God. "My meat," He said in one place, "is to do the will of Him that sent Me." This was life to Him. Sounds a bit like Paul, "To me to live is Christ" (Phil. 1:21). Jesus meant, "To Me to live is the Father." He sounds like Paul in other ways too, "The works that I do are not mine, but the Father which dwelleth in Me." Paul would say, "Not I but Christ that dwelleth in me." Jesus talked like any Christian might. He walked as Christians should. In fact, that's just what He is — **the first Christian!**

There is one way, however, in which He is not like any other Christian, and here we hasten to add the remainder of the verse quoted above; ". . . was tempted in all points like as we, **YET WITHOUT SIN."** That's not like any other Christian. Jesus could say, "I do **ALWAYS** those things that please Him" (John 8:29b). In all of His life He never once yielded to His humanity in spite of every pressure put upon Him by Satan. His life was flawless; fully victorious over every temptation. The "surrender arrow," if we may refer to our visual, was never once pointed toward the "spirit of man."

Some Christians, when first exposed to the doctrine of Christ's two natures, shrink from the fact that He possessed our human nature alongside the immaculate divine nature produced by the Holy Spirit. This is certainly understandable. Jesus Christ is so precious to us we don't like to think of His even soiling His hands. His perfection is so exalted in our minds that we would remove Him from any contact with man whatsoever. Of course, this is very natural for us. What is helpful in such a case is to remember that **temptation is not sin.** In the life of no one is temptation ever regarded as sin; **yielding** to it, is. Having a human nature is not sin, either. God does not indict man for possession of a human nature: that is not sin; but yielding to it is.

There's no damage done to the person of Jesus when we say that He was born with two natures; one the product of the flesh and the other the Spirit. As long as we are careful to say that He never once yielded to the human, His sinlessness and Deity are both untouched. What a wonderful Saviour it makes Him to be! His Saviourhood is marvelously enhanced when we see this truth. He knows exactly what we go through in life: not by reading it out of a book or producing from His omniscience — He knows by **experience.** He's been through it all Himself. He has endured, personally, everything that this life brings to us.

THE VICTORY OF CHRIST

The Bible turns the spotlight on Jesus' struggle of the two natures by recording His prayer battle in Gethsemane (Matt. 26:36-46). Hours before the cross we find Him in one of the most intense moments of His testings. We are permitted to see something of the contest of His natures and the great strain that it produced within His soul. How He felt the "tug-o-war!" "My soul is exceeding sorrowful, even unto death . . ." He said, as He confessed the great burden that the Spirit-flesh contest pressed down upon Him (Matt. 26:38). If there was ever a time when we would be permitted to see the great testing that Jesus endured for us, it is here. In Gethsemane the strain was tremendous — God, learning by experience the enormous power and attraction that sin has for men, groaned within Himself as He faced up to the decision. What a dreadful time it must have been for our dear

Saviour. Both of His natures pleading for the soul's decision. Everything depended upon this fateful moment. His life of obedience had now come to its climax — man's future fellowship with God was at stake.

In no way did the "first Adam" endure such agony. The Scripture, in giving us a full account, testifies, "And being in agony He prayed more earnestly: and His sweat as it were great drops of blood falling down to the ground" (Luke 22:44). You and I can't decide whether to watch television or pray, but here the powers of darkness and the armies of light waged their conflict on the battlefield of Christ's soul. Satan had access to His will through man's nature, exerting all pressure that he might cause Jesus to yield to the flesh and turn from the cross. The Holy Spirit, who also had access to His soul through the new or spiritual nature, constantly revealed to Him the perfect will of the Father and offered Him the power He needed for obedience. The flesh lusted against the Spirit and the Spirit against the flesh, as Paul put it, and the two were contrary one to the other (Gal. 5:17).

Matthew records the matter was not settled until Jesus had thrice dealt with the decision. After the first encounter, He emerged from the garden to declare to His disciples, "The spirit indeed is willing (intellectual assent to the will of God) but the flesh is weak (the pull of the flesh is almost overpowering)" (Matt. 26:41). Jesus hadn't read that someplace — He had just been through an experience which showed Him how weak the flesh really is. It is so weak that after one has spent whole nights in prayer — after one has lived a whole lifetime surrendered to the will of God — in a garden of Gethsemane one still has to sweat drops of blood before He can say, "Not My will but Thine be done." What a Man! What a Saviour! Could it be reverently said that Jesus had "guts"!

"Oh my Father, if it be possible, let this cup pass from Me: (that's what the old nature wanted) nevertheless

140

not as I will (notice the two contrasting wills), but as Thou wilt" (Matt. 26:39). He didn't pray that just one time. He had to deal with the "surrender arrow" three times before the matter was settled. Finally, it was over. The battle was won there in Gethsemane. That's where the victory of Christ was obtained — in prayer. The battle was not won at the cross — it was won in the garden. The victory was **displayed** at Calvary. The cross, raised in glory suspended the **triumphant** Christ between heaven and earth. This was an open triumph over the principalities and powers (Col. 2:15). The cross was not a place of shame for Jesus: it was a trophy of His final victory. The race was won. He crossed the tape a righteous man. Not a spot of sin was to be found in Him. He was declared, in this final act, to be perfect.

With His work in the body now finished He uttered the last words, "Father, into Thy hands I commend My Spirit." The atonement was completed. The righteousness man needed for the heavenly state was now assured. Jesus could resume His former glory. The self-emptying was over. He had accomplished what he had come to do. Now He could make the transition from the flesh to the spirit. The world would never again see Him as the humble carpenter's son. The next time the masses behold Him, He will be fully robed with all of the majesty and attributes of Deity. Sin has had its chance and failed. It could not conquer the Son of God. What a victory!

When a person bows his head and says, "Come into my heart, Lord Jesus," it is this same victorious Christ that enters. The same One who has personally faced everything that we will ever face: the same One who has dealt with every temptation and was never once defeated: He it is, that enters. It is His nature that we acquire when we are saved. It is Christ's victorious nature that makes up our "new man"— that's why John says that He "cannot sin" (I John 3:9). How blessed this is: the victory of Christ becoming ours when we yield to the new nature.

141

In the moment we submit to the indwelling Saviour, Satan becomes a "whipped dog." This is why dramatically (and probably excitedly) Paul declares, "We are more than conquerors **through** Him that loved us." How precious; when we yield to the "Spirit of Christ" we manifest not only the Lord's personality, but His victory as well. We become the Lord's "Pennsylvania Avenue." America salutes her outstanding heroes with ticker tape parades on this famous street, but our lives become the Lord's victory car. The cross displayed His triumph to the heavenlies, our lives manifest it to the world!

CHRIST THE FIRST CHRISTIAN

MAIN TEACHING (Review and Remember)

1. God became flesh by laying aside His glory and taking on human form (Phil. 2:6-8).

2. Jesus was born with two natures. From Mary He received His human nature and from the Holy Spirit, His divine nature (Luke 1:28-38).

3. As the first Christian, Christ became the Pioneer of our faith (Heb. 12:2).

4. His human nature permitted Him to be fully tempted "in all points yet without sin," while His divine nature made it possible for Him to do the righteous will of God.

5. He can be our example because His resources were the same as ours (Heb. 5:7-10).

6. His greatest test came at Gesthemane where the conflict of His two natures is clearly seen (Luke 22:39-46).

7. While the battle was won in the garden, the victory was displayed at the cross.

8. The victorious Christ became the "Life-giving Spirit" via the cross (1 Cor. 15:45; 2 Cor. 3:17,18).

9. When we receive Jesus, we receive the "Victor;" when we surrender to Him, we have His victory.

10. Our victorious lives display His personally won righteousness.

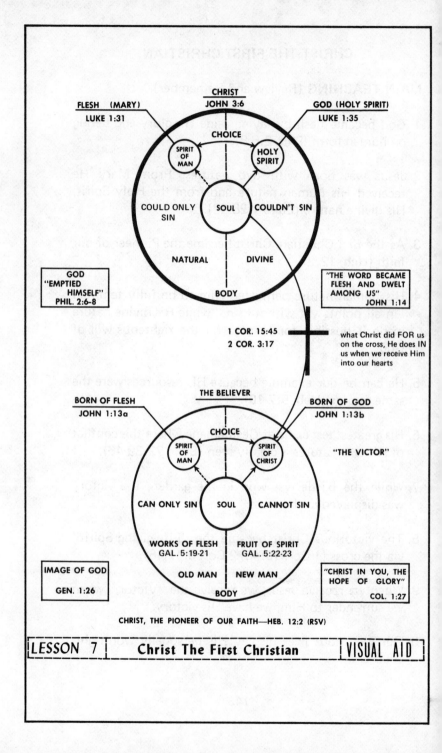

CHRIST
JOHN 3:6

FLESH (MARY)
LUKE 1:31

GOD (HOLY SPIRIT)
LUKE 1:35

CHOICE

SPIRIT OF MAN

HOLY SPIRIT

COULD ONLY SIN

SOUL

COULDN'T SIN

NATURAL

DIVINE

BODY

GOD "EMPTIED HIMSELF" PHIL. 2:6-8

"THE WORD BECAME FLESH AND DWELT AMONG US" JOHN 1:14

1 COR. 15:45
2 COR. 3:17

what Christ did FOR us on the cross, He does IN us when we receive Him into our hearts

THE BELIEVER

BORN OF FLESH
JOHN 1:13a

BORN OF GOD
JOHN 1:13b

CHOICE

SPIRIT OF MAN

SPIRIT OF CHRIST

"THE VICTOR"

CAN ONLY SIN

SOUL

CANNOT SIN

WORKS OF FLESH
GAL. 5:19-21

FRUIT OF SPIRIT
GAL. 5:22-23

IMAGE OF GOD
GEN. 1:26

OLD MAN

NEW MAN

BODY

"CHRIST IN YOU, THE HOPE OF GLORY" COL. 1:27

CHRIST, THE PIONEER OF OUR FAITH—HEB. 12:2 (RSV)

| LESSON 7 | Christ The First Christian | VISUAL AID |

CHAPTER EIGHT

THE SONSHIP OF THE BELIEVER

We have seen Jesus Christ as our self-emptied God coming to man's rescue. Equipped with two natures, the Second Adam was able to experience every temptation and trial of life. By the grace of God he never once yielded even though it was necessary for Him to taste death in the course of His perfect obedience. The sinless victor became the "life-giving Spirit" that men might have Him and be freed from sin's fatal grasp. His victory is relived through those persons who make Him Lord of their lives.

In the course of our study thus far, we have noted two reasons why God appeared in human form. First, that man who is cut off from the spirit world might know the true character of his maker. Jesus is the perfect revelation of the Father; the love of Jesus, as well as His forgiveness, is truly that of God. This is the content of His words, "He that hath seen Me hath seen the Father" (John 14:9). Secondly, since God chose to redeem man at the very point where the fall occurred, He came in the role of the Second Adam to effect our redemption. This aspect of Jesus' ministry is sometimes called the atonement. It includes, not only His triumph over Satan in the garden and on the cross, but His indwelling of the believer. It is His coming into men's hearts that really accomplishes the restoration of man to God. He is both the revelation of the Father and the Redeemer of man.

THE PROCESS OF THE NEW BIRTH

In this chapter we are to examine the actual mechanics of the new birth. Previously, we have spoken of men as becoming the "born-again" sons of God upon receipt of the Holy Spirit. Now we are to explore the matter more fully as we plunge deeper into the fascinating truth of salvation.

It is always exciting to inspect truths that have to do with our own situation. The object of our study just now is something that is part of our present experience: it must mean more to us than mere words on a page. It is more than theory — it is a present joy.

Chapter three introduced us to the beginning of this marvelous process. There we noted that Jesus is literally received by the believer and that divine sonship is produced by that experience. Now we are to continue the story and learn its intriguing finish. The process is not hard to understand because physical life furnishes us with a practical visual aid. The reproduction process which takes place in the natural realm has an interesting parallel in the spirit. Almost everyone is familiar with the steps involved in passing physical life from one generation to another: i.e., conception, prenatal (pregnancy) period, followed by birth or delivery. For any species to reproduce itself there must be these steps.

This is not true just of the physical creation alone, but is also found to occur in the spiritual realm as well. That which is true of human reproduction is also true with respect to the spiritual reproduction of the family of God. For men to become the sons of God, a complete reproductive process is needed. There must be conception, a prenatal or development period followed by the birth or delivery.

When the Bible refers to our being born of God or as the sons of God, it envisions the whole process rather than the individual steps within the process. We do the same. When we speak of bearing children or having children, we are not referring just to the conception or the carrying of the child, but to the whole procedure. The Bible describes the Christian as God's child even though all of the steps of his production have not yet been completed. The apostles John and Paul both delight in referring to the saints as the sons of God. Paul exhorts us to "walk as becometh the sons of God," and John insists, "Beloved now are we the sons of God."

Jesus words to Nicodemus offer good insight to the subject. Concerning spiritual life, He teaches, ". . . except a man be born again he cannot see the kingdom of God" (John 3:3). Our attention is directed to the word "born." Here the original language is required to give the exact meaning. The subject is not really birth at all for the verb "Gennao" as used here has to do with **fathering** or **begetting.** It could just as easily read, "except a man be brought into existence or sired again . . ." Jesus is talking to Nicodemus about starting life all over again from the **conception** stage. "Except a man be conceived again he cannot see the kingdom of God" is a more appropriate way for us to handle the Lord's words for this is surely His meaning. "Born again," as used here, can be properly understood as referring to spiritual conception: the point at which one begins the new life as a child of God.

 Nicodemus understands this to be the significance of Christ's words. He does not see how it is possible, but he is well aware of the implication of the statement he's just heard. He knows that a new conception is referred to for he asks, ". . .can he enter the second time into his mother's **womb** and be born?" (John 3:4). We know that our interpretation of Jesus' words is correct for Nicodemus understands the Lord to be speaking of conception and pregnancy. What Nicodemus missed, however, was that Jesus was not talking of a second **physical** conception, but a **spiritual** one. Man needs to be conceived again to become God's son, but not of the flesh. He needs to be conceived by the Holy Spirit.

147

Jesus points this out to Nicodemus; "That which is born of the flesh is flesh, and that which is born of the Spirit is spirit." Poor Nic, his mind was not used to spiritual things even though he was a spiritual leader in Israel. He bewilderingly asks, "How can these things be?" His thinking was limited to the natural realm only, so a second birth posed a physical impossibility. When John later refers to this matter in his epistle we see that sexual language is employed, "Whosoever is born of God doth not commit sin; for His (God's) seed remaineth in him . . ." (I John 3:9). God's seed in man is clearly a reproductive feature: conception is certainly envisioned here.

If what has been pointed out is so, then Jesus' words to Nicodemus have the force of, "While your mother and father were involved in your first birth — (natural generation), it is the Holy Spirit and the Word of God that will effect your spiritual regeneration. You must have a second conception if you hope to see the kingdom of God. Just as you needed a physical birth to appear on earth, so also do you need a spiritual birth to appear in heaven."

There is a sense in which we can say that the Christian is one who is pregnant with the life of God. Just as the sperm and ovum unite in physical union to form a new creation, so also when the Holy Spirit (Spirit of Christ) is literally joined to the soul of a man, there is a new creation. A spiritual pregnancy occurs that is akin to the physical one, and it is just as real. It takes place with the same speed, too. In the instant one opens the door of his heart to the Lord a spiritual pregnancy occurs in that same second. It can occur but once to produce a physical life and it occurs but once to produce a spiritual life.

The imagination becomes a blessed tool when it is able to comprehend and picture spiritual truths. The truth of divine sonship comes to life when we can think of our bodies as being a huge womb. The spiritual pregnancy that takes place with the decision of salvation allows a new person (the new man) to be conceived within the body-womb. This person lives for a time in that womb. Thus it is that the Christian life, becomes the "womb-stage" for the maturing infant son of God. Our lives on earth, after the conception, correspond to the prenatal period of the physical process. The little new man is allowed to develop for a time before his actual delivery. Every Christian reading these lines is in that prenatal stage now; the time of his delivery is yet future.

Even though we are in the pre-delivery stage our sonship is not marred by that fact. We are as truly the sons of God this moment as we will ever be. When John says, "Beloved now are we the sons of God . . . ," he means right now. Sonship is not something that belongs to the future. Even though a woman is carrying her child it is just as much her child before delivery as after. He does not suddenly become more her child after he is delivered. True, she may not know as much about him, but she does know that he is her baby. He is probably already named and plans are laid for his care and training. The fact that the mother does not know the sex of the child, whether it is a boy or girl, doesn't mar his sonship at all: the child is still hers. John speaks the same of the Christian, ". . . now are we the sons of God, but it doth not yet appear what we shall be . . ." While we are in the womb-stage others know very little about us. We remain unseen until the time of our delivery, then we shall be known even as we are also known by God (I Cor. 13:12).

One thing is certain, however, when we finally emerge from the womb we will be like our parent. That's the law of the harvest. John offers the same, ". . . it doth not yet appear what we shall be, but we know that when He shall appear, we shall **be like Him** . . ." (I John 3:2). The child must be like his parents. Since we are born of Christ, we must be like Him.

Our prenatal period (earthly life) is a time of growth and development. Even as the baby develops within the mother's womb, so the Christian life permits maturation. The prenatal development must precede the actual delivery. Each of us then, is awaiting that future "blessed event." It will be a time of manifesting or revealing; a time when we will be displayed as the sons of God. It is an occasion, says Paul, for which the whole creation is waiting, "For the earnest expectation of the creation **waiteth for the revealing of the sons of God**" (Rom. 8:19). Someone has written, "The world is waiting for the sunrise." The Bible asserts that the manifesting of the sons of God is the great day for which the creation longs. Eternity will truly begin for us in that yet future time when the family of God is gloriously unveiled.

THE THREE STAGES OF OUR SONSHIP

RECEIVE CHRIST (new nature) NEW BABE	TWO NATURES PRODUCE CHRISTIAN GROWTH (maturity)	REVEALED AS SONS —APPEAR WITH CHRIST IN GLORY
CONCEPTION (pregnant with God's life)	PRENATAL PERIOD (gestation time)	DELIVERY (adoption)

While we generally think of being "born-again" as a single experience, it actually comes about in three stages. The moment we receive Christ we become pregnant with the life of God. Then follows the gestation period lasting as long as our life on earth. Finally "D Day" (delivery day) comes when we are displayed to the world as God's sons. These three stages are lumped as one when we refer to a person as being "born-again."

In the same instant of our conception as the sons of God we are guaranteed the delivery. When Jesus enters the human heart, that individual is simultaneously sealed and guaranteed to stand before God as one of His redeemed. This is a conception that is safe from miscarriage. The new creation that comes into being (new man) belongs to God. There is no power that can take him away; no sickness, disease or accident can remove him. The work of the Holy Spirit cannot be undone. There is nothing that can uncreate something that God has created. No, once the reproduction has begun it is guaranteed to end in a safe delivery.

Note: The question might be asked whether or not the new creation can be aborted. The answer is no. The new creation is perfect. It is conceived by God. There is no reason for an abortion to occur. As to whether or not an abortion could be performed, that is from the outside, then the one performing the abortion would have to be more powerful than God. Satan would like to abort the new creation, but he does not have that kind of power. God very clearly says, "Neither shall any man pluck them out of My hand" (John 10:28). Suppose, however, that an abortion was possible. This would mean that the fetus, once aborted could never be put back. But if it is to go back into the same womb, why abort in the first place?

Some Christians worry because they can't FEEL their salvation. They are uneasy because no **physical** signs attest to the sonship. They long supernatural phenomena which will certify their spiritual pregnancy. These people can never be satisfied. They will always be troubled. The truth is, spiritual conception cannot be detected by any fleshly means. That is, salvation cannot be felt, seen, tasted, or heard. But that doesn't mean there

151

are no signs of life. Indeed there are. The new man makes his presence known with three distinct changes in the believer's life; (1) he acquires a love for the brethren; (2) he acquires a hunger for God's Word and will; (3) he experiences an inner witness of the Spirit to his heart (1 John 5:10). To insist that physical manifestations are needed to confirm a person's salvation, will immediately rob a Christian of both his security and joy.

Emotionalism has an important and necessary place in the Christian religion because we are emotional beings, but to insist on emotional signs of one's salvation is to confuse the flesh with the spirit. The writer does not condemn those who hold to such views, but suggests that insight and understanding could bring a release and satisfaction to their Christian experience. Freeing the sign-seeker from his fruitless quest can fill his life with even greater joy in Christ.

There are days when mothers, in the early months of their pregnancy, feel nothing at all. They carry on all sorts of vigorous activities with almost no regard for "their condition." They go hiking, camping, work at their jobs; often forgetting the fact that they are going to have a baby. Yet, irrespective of how they **feel,** they nonetheless are pregnant. The conception has occurred. Feelings of one kind or another can never alter the fact. Feeling never alters fact. True it is then, if a person has genuinely opened the door of his heart to Jesus, the new man is conceived and **spiritual** signs of his presence can be expected as the new creation develops.

THE NATURE OF THE DELIVERY

The future delivery of the Christian has a special name in Scripture. It is called the **adoption.** When the delivery or adoption takes place the **process** of producing God's sons is finally completed. The term "adoption," as scripturally employed, does not have the same meaning it popularly

152

conveys. Today, adoption has to do with the legal process of **becoming** a man's son. The judge signs a paper and one is legally declared to be the child of a person who was not his parent. Biblically, however, the term has to do with the manifesting or revealing of one who is **already** a son of God. It has nothing to do with **becoming** a son; only with being **revealed** as a son. It is the final stage of a process that had long since begun. Paul's use of the word is misunderstood when it is treated in the popular sense. He teaches the Romans, ". . . but ye have received the Spirit of adoption, whereby we cry, Abba, Father" (Rom. 8:15b). Sometimes Christians, having this very verse in mind, will pray, "Lord, we thank Thee that we have been adopted into your family." These dear ones mean well, but they do not understand the Bible's meaning of the expression. The verse doesn't say that we're adopted; it says only that we have received the "Spirit" of adoption.

No one is adopted into the family of God; that is, not in the popular sense. Christians are **born** into the family of God; they become sons by birth, not by any legal process. Just as men become the children of their parents by a process of conception and birth, so also do they become the sons of God. He is the true parent of His offspring. Never once is it hinted in the Word that we are God's sons by any other means. The concept of the second birth would be utterly destroyed by a doctrine of legal adoption.

". . . Ye have received the Spirit of adoption . . ." is but another way of saying, "ye have received the Holy Spirit." The Spirit of God is given many names in the Bible and this is one. Here He is called the "Spirit of adoption" because it has reference to His function of guaranteeing the adoption event. When He teaches us the Word of God He is called the "Spirit of truth," etc.

What does adoption mean then? Paul is using the word in the sense in which it was employed in his day. He was referring to the Roman custom by which sons were

153

officially declared to have reached manhood. When a boy reached twenty-one his father would take him to the market place and he would be ceremoniously exhibited and acknowledged as an adult. From thenceforth he was regarded as a man in his own right and could negotiate business. This is very much as we acknowledge our young people by allowing them to vote and sign contracts. Paul is thinking in terms of the ceremonial process and is anticipating the day when the sons of God will be displayed in their maturity.

Everyone receives the "Spirit of adoption" when he is saved, but no person on earth is yet manifested. Here then is the distinction; we receive the "Spirit of adoption" upon salvation, but the adoption does not occur until we have put off the robe of flesh. It is a future step that awaits all Christians who are on the earth. Note Paul's words, ". . . we ourselves groan within ourselves, **waiting for our adoption,** to wit, the redemption of our body" (Rom. 8:23b). Thus we find that adoption is but the final step in God's reproductive system.

Note: Our adoption includes two appearances: (1) when death strikes our physical bodies and we make the transition from flesh to spirit, we first appear in our heavenly body, the ETERNAL form. We are then manifested to all those who entered heaven ahead of us. (2) Our second appearance occurs when the Lord returns to earth in His glorified body. We will appear with Him wearing a glorified PHYSICAL body like His. Then all those who are on earth will see that we are the Sons of God. Paul has this second manifestation in mind when he says we are "waiting eagerly for our adoption as sons, the redemption of our body" (Rom. 8:23). The adoption which has to do with the redeemed body takes place on earth at Jesus' return with ALL His saints (I Thess. 3:13).

Let's observe the steps in order. First, the Holy Spirit comes into our lives and the new man is conceived: that is **CONCEPTION.** We remain on the earth after salvation so that the new man has a chance to grow and develop; that is the **PRENATAL** stage. The delivery of the new man occurs after we make the transition from flesh to spirit. Thus the putting off of our bodies is really the time of **ADOPTION.** The soul, after release from the body, stands clothed in the form of Christ and all the saints are revealed to each other. That is the real new birth of the Christian; that's when he appears; that is when he emerges from the womb-stage and is clearly identified as God's child.

 Adoption is the **result** of conception and it is guaranteed as we have seen. The **process** of our birth is most interesting. The illustration of seed-life serves wonderfully in making the truth simple. The life of a seed is encased within the shell and it must remain there until released. It cannot be seen until that seed is planted and watered. Then the shell deteriorates and the new creation is allowed to come forth. The same is true of the Christian. The life is encased within the body-shell, but it cannot be manifested until that shell has been dissolved—this dissolution is physical death.

Our bodies, like the mother's womb, are **prisons in** one sense, for the new creation cannot be **revealed until** released. The same is true of **seeds as demonstrated by** the kernels of corn taken from King Tut's tomb. **After** being stored for thousands of years, these kernels, **when** planted and watered, produced beautiful stalks **and full** ears of corn. The life that was imprisoned **remained there**

155

until released by the dissolution of the outer case. Jesus used this same figure in speaking of His own forthcoming death, ". . . Except a grain of wheat fall into the earth and die, it abideth alone, but if it die, it beareth much fruit" (John 12:24).

This is the process of our coming delivery. The life is encased within the physical body until death comes, then it is released and the person inside can be displayed in the presence of God. Instead of being the great blight and terror that plagues men's souls, death is now seen as the exciting transition from the dark womb stage. The new creation (the Christian) suddenly blossoms into the true life for which he was originally designed. Paul speaks of this adoption event in another way; "For we know that if the earthly house of our tabernacle be dissolved, we have a building from God, a house not made with hands, eternal in the heavens" (2 Cor. 5:1). When this occurs, the birth process is complete and we are ready to begin eternity in the presence of God: to be absent from the body is to be present with the Lord.

Some reading these lines might feel that since the delivery is yet future the Christian is somehow incomplete until that day arrives. In truth, the Christian is complete from the moment of his conception. The delivery or mani- festation will not add to his person in any way. The child that is carried in his mother's womb is complete. Doctors and geneticists inform us that the characteristics and struc- ture of one's physical make-up is determined the instant the ovum is fertilized. The color of the hair and eyes as well as many traits are fully established in that same moment. So it is with the Christian; he is complete from the time the Holy Spirit is united with the soul. True, time is needed for his development, but nothing is missing from his per- son. Everything that will appear before God is a part of the conception and needs only maturation. The child of God is "complete in Him," says Paul (Col. 2:10).

Note: When physical death occurs and we are ADOPTED as God's sons, ALL GROWTH of our persons as we now know it—ENDS. Once we are delivered from our physical bodies, we cease to grow in the Lord's likeness. In this aspect, the spiritual birth process is **not like** the physical birth process. Both the human child and plants continue to grow after they are manifested to the world. **We do not.** Once death releases us from the struggle of our two natures, we are all through growing in the likeness of the Lord. We have just this one lifetime to become like Jesus. You'll see why when we come to chapter ten.

SUMMARY OF THE PROCESS

Referring to the printed visual of the lesson we see the entire system of reproducing the sons of God. First, we note God the Eternal Spirit in heaven. He is invisible to men. Then God became visible in Jesus Christ so that men could see Him and know Him. In the days of His flesh, Jesus produced within Himself the righteousness that men need for the eternal fellowship. By means of the cross He became the life-giving Spirit so that men could have His righteousness and be equipped for heaven. He is now invisible.

We, on earth, receive the "life-giving Spirit" and a new creation (new man) is conceived by that union. After a time in the flesh, in which the victory of Christ makes it possible for men to live unto God and grow through the two-nature struggle, the new man is ready to stand before God. The flesh, or physical clothing, falls away and the child stands before God in the spirit ready for his life proper. His departure from the earthly womb-stage is called the "adoption." Thus the divine reproduction system has been unfolded. This is not just a Bible theory, but a process that is taking place within each child of God this very minute. In spite of the cold manner in which truth comes from the pages of a book, here is a warm, vital experience that is true of each person who has received Jesus Christ as his Saviour. We are as much the sons of God now as we'll ever be, and His passion for us and devotion to us will never be any greater. He loves us with a holy and pure love that transcends anything we can hope to give those who are born of us. This is why we sing, "Love divine, all love excelling, Joy of heaven, to earth come down."

THE SONSHIP OF THE BELIEVER

MAIN TEACHING (Review and Remember)

1. God is an invisible Spirit. He became flesh in order to reveal Himself to man and to redeem him. At the cross He became the invisible Spirit again so that men might have Him.

2. Any birth, physical or spiritual, has three phases: conception, prenatal, and delivery.

3. The difference between flesh and spirit is emphasized as Jesus talks to Nicodemus about spiritual conception (John 3:1-6).

4. With one's decision for Christ, a spiritual conception instantly takes place.

5. Our Christian lives may be likened to the prenatal development of an infant—a future delivery awaits (Ro. 8:19).

6. The Holy Spirit, Himself, is our guarantee of a safe delivery (Eph. 4:30; 2 Cor. 5:5).

7. The Bible calls the delivery that occurs after physical death, "the adoption" (Ro. 8:15b; Ro. 8:23). Illustration: Roman custom.

8. The **process** of the delivery is like that of the seed which contains a life that is released only upon deterioration of the outer case.

9. As the seed holds all the future features, so are we complete the moment we receive Christ (Col. 2:10).

10. The moment we are released from these bodies (physical death), we appear in the presence of Christ (2 Cor. 5:8). Our adoption is our manifestation in the new form after this present one is dissolved.

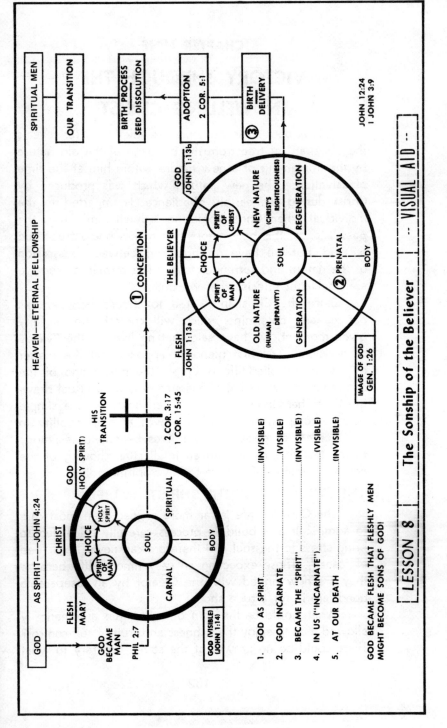

HEAVEN—ETERNAL FELLOWSHIP

SPIRITUAL MEN

OUR TRANSITION

BIRTH PROCESS
SEED DISSOLUTION

ADOPTION
2 COR. 5:1

③ BIRTH
DELIVERY

JOHN 12:24
1 JOHN 3:9

① CONCEPTION

THE BELIEVER

GOD
JOHN 1:13b

SPIRIT
OF
CHRIST

NEW NATURE
(CHRIST'S
RIGHTEOUSNESS)

CHOICE

SOUL

REGENERATION

SPIRIT
OF
MAN

OLD NATURE
(HUMAN
DEPRAVITY)

② PRENATAL

BODY

FLESH
JOHN 1:13a

GENERATION

IMAGE OF GOD
GEN. 1:26

GOD AS SPIRIT——JOHN 4:24

CHRIST

GOD
(HOLY SPIRIT)

HIS
TRANSITION

2 COR. 3:17
1 COR. 15:45

FLESH
MARY

CHOICE

HOLY
SPIRIT

SPIRITUAL

(INVISIBLE)

GOD
BECAME MAN
PHIL 2:7

SPIRIT
OF MAN

SOUL

CARNAL

BODY

GOD (VISIBLE)
(JOHN 1:14)

GOD   AS SPIRIT   (INVISIBLE)

1. GOD AS SPIRIT .... (INVISIBLE)

2. GOD INCARNATE .... (VISIBLE)

3. BECAME THE "SPIRIT" .... (INVISIBLE)

4. IN US ("INCARNATE") .... (VISIBLE)

5. AT OUR DEATH .... (INVISIBLE)

GOD BECAME FLESH THAT FLESHLY MEN
MIGHT BECOME SONS OF GOD!

| LESSON 8 | The Sonship of the Believer | -- VISUAL AID -- |

CHAPTER NINE

VICTORY THROUGH THE INDWELLING CHRIST

A look back over the course traveled thus far reveals the Christian set free from the bondage of the old nature by the implanting of a new nature within him at the time of salvation. The new nature, which was produced by Christ during His earthly obedience, is imparted to the individual when Christ comes to indwell him. It is the **possession** of this holy nature that makes one a true child of God, but we have distinguished between possession of the nature and surrender to it. The former is who we are: the latter effects what we do.

Since the Christian is free to choose between his natures and determine which will control him for any given moment, we have said that he lives in the "valley of decision." At first glance it appears that the matter of a God-controlled life is simply the positioning of the surrender arrow. What appears so easy on a visual drawing is far harder in the life. What looks to be a simple pencil stroke on paper often proves an impossibility in the moment of decision. Our lives bear loud testimony to the fact that more than an intellectual shoving of the arrow is required if we are to have Spirit-led lives.

THE STRUGGLE OF THE CHRISTIAN LIFE

The Christian life is far more rugged than most care to admit. It is a building process carefully calculated to bring stress to the soul and therefore can never be a "bed of roses." Those expecting an easy time in life because they are now united with the Creator by an inseparable bond, are in for a rude shock.

What would be the gain of a life that automatically allowed men to enjoy the richness and fruit of self-control? There could be no growth of the soul. Contrary to what most Christians suppose, having Christ does not guarantee that a person's life **will** change at all; it guarantees only that one's life **can** change. There is no automatic fruit-bearing after one comes to God. That life remains the stewardship of the individual. He is responsible for any changes that occur. God's will for one's life can never override the Christian at any point: the result would not be obedience.

God provides a life of stress so that the Christian can grow in the likeness of Christ. God manipulates external circumstances so that the believer is perpetually faced with making a choice. It is the constant choosing in each situation that exercises the soul. Just as body muscles need exercise for development, so do our souls. Soul exercise produces the maturity that God desires in His children. This is the way He prepares them for future fellowship with Himself.

A person must work hard to develop a well-muscled body. It takes discipline and determination to build a nice body. It is no less easy to develop the soul into the likeness of Christ. It takes a lot of self-denial and watching for Satan. It takes power to tame the tongue and sacrifice the things of the world if one is to become like Jesus. The man who wants to be like Jesus must deny himself many things which are all right for other people, but damaging for those who care about building up the new man.

Our two natures are opposites. One is spiritual and the other is carnal. The chief difference between them is their respective appetites. One hungers for the things of God and the other hungers for material things and pleasures of life on earth. The former seeks to please God and the latter seeks to satisfy the fleshly instincts and impulses of man as an earth-bound creature. Were the two natures alike, there would be no contest for the believer. His soul would have no problem deciding which should control him. If for example, the new nature hungered for power and fame, why should the believer care who directed his steps in the pursuit of the goal. If it were money or sexual pleasure the same would be true. If on the other hand, both natures longed for prayer fellowship with the Father and had an insatiable thirst for the Bible, the believer would care little which nature directed him in achieving that satisfaction.

Our natures are **not** alike and therefore the believer must decide in every instance which shall have control. He must decide which appetite is to have the satisfaction that he is able to obtain for it. He must decide which will motivate his actions in attempting to reach satisfying goals. Thus, as long as we are in the body and possessed of two natures, we must make never ending choices. This is the way we mature.

If the Christian life were a matter of intellectual assent to the pleas of God's Spirit, there could be no question of our choice for obedience. We would, with our heads, choose to please Christ every time. We don't, however, and this is evidence that the struggle between our contrary natures requires more than head-nodding decisions. Elements of our own personality are brought into the conflict, and we find ourselves strangely **compelled** to do things that are not compatible with our reason. Sometimes it appears that the struggle of the two natures is better described as a battle between our hearts and our heads. Our emotions vie with our intellect for the mastery of our will.

Before salvation, our lives were lived exclusively under the control of one nature — the old man. The years of his exclusive domination depend, of course, on how early one is saved. During that time, the flow of one's life is geared to pleasing the depraved nature and satisfying self-centered demands. One's time, money, energies, in fact everything, is used to feed and exercise the Adamic nature so that the old man's growth and maturity come rapidly. Inasmuch as life on this planet is centered around fallen man (not God), the mode of living is that which best serves the interests of the fallen nature. The bulk of human existence is manifestly away from God. The news-papers, radios, movies, pleasures and entertainments are far from godly. The whole world ministers to depraved man for it is filled with self-seeking lost men. The God-seekers are few. The daily life routines are barely affected by their presence.

People are born into this God-opposing life stream and in a very short time become well adjusted to it. Their lives adopt a pattern which is shaped and moulded before they reach their teens. The ego drive, sex drive and social drive are fairly well crystallized by the time physical maturity is reached. The total personality gains momentum with the passing of years. The direction, of course, is dictated by the old nature.

When a man is saved and acquires a new nature, a whole new life is opened to him. It is a strange life and one which is unknown. It is completely different from anything that he has experienced so far. It has to do with a future that has no physical guarantee here on earth. It requires him to talk to a God whom he cannot see or hear. It asks that he turn from many things which once brought delight and satisfactions, temporary though they were. It commands him to speak to the God-opposing world of the Maker's love for all men. He is to encourage men to follow his example in abandoning the pursuit of worldly treasure and fame as he follows the example of One who died on a cross 2000 years ago.

The new life, instead of bringing comforts and feasting-pleasures, promises struggle and despisement for those who will truly dedicate themselves to it. It requires action on the basis of an Old Book and inward conviction alone. It promises its great rewards after one has died. This is the life that is opened to men because they have received the new nature. Surrender may not be so easy under such circumstances. Men are not used to living by unseen spirits and blind trust in a miracle-filled Book. This is a very mystifying thing regardless of the love and grace that bring it into one's life.

The two natures therefore offer two ways of life. One we are used to, and the other completely new and different. The Christian, in spite of the opportunity of the new life before him, cannot always bring himself to follow it even though he knows that it is the fulfillment of his destiny. Though convinced that any other course is tragic waste, the decision is beyond him. Salvation does open a new God-pleasing channel into which one may pour his life, but the Christian discovers that changing the stream is far from automatic. Salvation has made it possible for his life to flow in a new direction, but it does not **make** it do so. The momentum of the old life seems to prohibit any change and the power of the old man (old life) is very great. We are so accustomed to the old-life routine that the new Bible program takes on frightening unnaturalness.

As easy as the choice appears from our visual drawings, the unnatural character of Christian living makes for great difficulty in choosing. Participating in church fellowships, extended Bible study, prayer sessions, are foreign intrusions upon the life schedule. The loving of enemies and giving away our personal fortunes is certainly not the world's formula for success and happiness. The average person is busy seeking all he can get from his neighbor and life: not the reverse. The most natural process is to please self. It seems as if every demand inside us serves to keep us from that surrender to the indwelling Christ. Life itself seems arrayed against Christian responsibility so that yielding to the new man is the hardest job of the soul.

Note: Some believers think that Christianity has to do with belonging to a church and learning the Bible. This is a mistake. Bible knowledge is vital, but Christianity is a LIFE, not biblical theory. It has to do with CHANGES in a person. He must not be the same today as he was yesterday. God uses CIRCUMSTANCES to pressure us into Christ-like changes. Therefore Christianity has to do with bad working conditions, sassy children, mean neighbors, sickness and tragedy. God watches for your reactions in the midst of life's trials. Are you more patient today? Are you sweeter to your wife, pay your bills quicker, discipline your children more lovingly, drive your car better, and speak more kindly of others? Have you already decided to forsake family, fame and fortune because none of those have value where you're going? Do you want to make it big in heaven or on earth? That's what God wants to know. You answer by the way you LIVE.

The world about the Christian spins at a mad pace and sweeps men into its whirlpool of busy routine. Men tread the squirrel cage of three meals a day, on the job and back to bed, in an endless cycle. People are sucked down into the busy, busy, busy rotation of job, family, dishes, washing, car, trips, T.V. etc. It doesn't really matter what it is as long as they spend the vast energies of the human personality to survive. Even the Christian, though possessed of the new nature which can take him out of this whirling bog, scarcely has time to consider what God has done within him. Many are caught in the revolving-door-life that the "old man" has created, and are as one who has a million dollars in the bank but is too busy to write a check.

THE VICTORY IN LIFE THROUGH SURRENDER

What a tragedy when men, who have Christ's victorious nature, find themselves unwilling to yield to it. If only that surrender could be made. What a difference it would make. Just the simple shifting of the surrender arrow transforms everything for us. This is the key — shifting that arrow is an absolute necessity. This is what brings God's power into our life story. The moment we make the switch (the moment we make our surrender) all of the resources of heaven act to overcome the "gravity-pull" of the old life. It is like throwing a "reverse switch" on an electric motor. The enormous power of the Holy One energizes the personality in a God-pleasing direction so that the victory of Christ is manifested in the believer's walk.

God leaves that arrow alone. How many times have we said that? It's so true though, we are the one's that make the surrender to Him. He supplies the power. That which results is similar to a phenomenon reported by a national magazine in covering the scene of a recent tornado. A picture accompanying the article showed a piece of straw driven through a telephone pole. The straw, so weak by itself, was surrendered to the wind. This surrender made the power of the wind the power of the straw. Our surrender to the indwelling Christ does the same for us.

We are so weak. We have no power within ourselves. Any talk of fighting sin or self reformation is inadmissible. If we are honest with ourselves, we will acknowledge that we prefer the things of the old life. Certainly our life investment seems to indicate that. We really haven't a chance against Satan's wiles. We desperately need our Saviour's mighty delivering hand. Our heads tell us we must yield to Christ; our emotions say, "Don't do it." Yet in the instant of our decision to surrender, His victory, that same victory that has conquered everything that this life can hurl against a person, becomes instantly and automatically operative. We must remind ourselves that this is not a once-for-all decision — it is moment by moment walking with Jesus. It may last but a fraction of a second, yet in that fraction we have Jesus' victory. The rest of the time we do not.

How wonderful it would be if we could surrender to Him all of the time! Our lives would be filled with the things of God, knowing His constant presence. The great passion of our souls would not be for the things of the world, but for God's own person. The force of our total personalities would move toward Him. What glory that would be! It was true of Jesus. Everything in His life was geared **away from** the course of the world. What a miracle that would be in us! It is a miracle when anything occurs to stem the rushing tide of our busy lives. Christians who stop attending church for a month are amazed to note how quickly they drift into the ways of the world. It takes supernatural power to halt the dashing members of a family long enough to have family altar — even if it were but three minutes a day. How different it would be, though, if we could give Him that surrender.

The victory we seek is illustrated by the story of a man who learned a wonderful Christian lesson from a fig tree in his back yard. He had pruned the tree one season, and allowed one of the branches to remain upon the ground for some time. Coming back to the tree some weeks later, he noticed that the leaves were still attached to the fallen branch. He glanced at the tree, and seeing the leaves were all gone from the other branches, wondered why they did not fall from the pruned branch as well. He pulled at the leaves on the branch and was surprised to find them still fast and requiring some effort to tear them loose. Then suddenly the truth dawned upon him. Leaves do not fall off a tree. They are pushed out by the indwelling life to make room for new growth and fruit.

The simple observation of this man beautifully highlights the truth of Christ's victory in our lives. It's true that the tree did not have a choice in the fruit it was to bear: the fact that it had but one nature settled that. It could bear only one kind of fruit. The Christian, however, can bear two kinds, for he has two natures and can choose. When the Christian decides to live for Christ and surrenders to the indwelling Spirit, the fruit of the Spirit appears. The crowding out of sin from His life is like the leaves on the fig tree: it is pushed out by the life of the indwelling Lord. The lesson teaches that we should get as close to Christ as possible: be surrendered to Him as much as possible and allow His victory to remove the dead leaves of the former life. It is Christ that deals with the "sin-leaves," not us.

Victory, then, comes as we get close to Christ. We must make it our business to be aware of Him and fellowship with Him as we go about the routine matters of each day. But this is not so easy. The moment a Christian tries, he finds he has a fight on his hands. The last thing the devil wants is for a Christian to fix his mind on the Lord. He knows what that can produce. He doesn't want believers close to Christ so he moves to prevent it. This explains the real struggle of the Christian life.

Note: In order that this chapter might stay focused on getting close to the Lord, I have not discussed the negative side of Christian victory. We have a powerful and persistent enemy. There can be no lasting victory until we learn how to deal with him. However, dealing with the devil is a separate matter, one which I treat fully in another book. In the appendix you will find a discussion on the part resisting the devil plays in our victory over sin.

There's a difference in **kind** between the old man and the new man. Our surrender choice is between two very different types of men. One is a man (nature) of **feeling** who walks by sight. The other is a man (nature) of **fact,** who walks by faith. They appear much the same on our visual, because it is difficult to represent feeling and fact visually. The old man we know very well. He is no stranger to us. Everything about him fills our awareness and we can please him by dipping into the world's supply of goods and pleasures. He feeds on physical delights. The new man is virtually a stranger. His cravings take us into a different world: a world of unseen things where spiritual delights are appropriated by faith. Thus the real handicap and main hindrance to Christian surrender now becomes clear.

There is no power within man to MAKE him obey fact. Man does not heartily respond to knowledge. We are emotional beings. The powers within us are geared largely to our feelings, not facts. All of our appetites, instincts, and passions are directed by how we **feel,** not by how we **think.** We do what we **want** to do many times more often than we do what we **ought** to do. We do pretty much what we feel like doing and when we feel like doing it. We pray when we get good and ready. We don't read the Bible unless we want to and there is no power within us to make us do it even when we know (with our heads) that we should. We do what we want to do. We are controlled by drives and appetites; not by our heads, as we might like to think. Men are not really intellectual beings; they are emotional beings who respond easily to feeling, and not to fact. Here then is the explanation of our difficulty in choosing surrender to Christ. His indwelling presence in our lives **IS FACT ALONE.** If there is no power within our being to **make us** respond to fact, then there is nothing within us to compel us to respond to Christ. If we are to have Christ's victory in our lives, we need to discover some way to respond to His presence.

CHRISTIAN VICTORY IS FOUND IN DEVELOPING AN AWARENESS OF CHRIST'S PRESENCE

We Cannot Detect Christ's Person

The decision at salvation brings a living person into our hearts. We literally receive the Person of Jesus, but He is Spirit. There is no physical form (body) for us to detect. We have no way of becoming aware of His presence by means of the senses, i.e., no way of touching, seeing or hearing Him. We know that He is in our hearts only because the Bible and the Holy Spirit have borne witness to the miracle. We are aware of the **FACT** OF HIS PRESENCE, but we are **not** aware of His person.

Paul's words, ". . . that Christ may dwell in your hearts **by faith,"** afford a genuine clue to our difficulty. He is telling us in clear language that it is by faith **we** understand that Jesus is spiritually united with us. The writer to the Hebrews employs similar thinking, "By faith, we **understand** that the worlds were framed by the Word of God . . ." (Heb. 11:3). By faith we have an understanding, says the writer, and from this we form our convictions. We hold these convictions in our heads. The Apostle John expresses himself in the same way, "And we know that the Son of God is come, and hath **given**

172

us an understanding . . ." (I John 5:20). It is through this understanding, he says, that we know Christ. Christ's presence within us therefore is known on the UNDERSTANDING level **only**. We **know** Him, but we cannot **feel** Him.

The **fact** of Christ's presence is a part of our working knowledge. We are convinced of His indwelling. We know of Him as much as we know the truth of Columbus. He landed on American shores in 1492 A.D. and this fact reposes within our understanding. We've never seen Columbus, but we are convinced that he lived. We hold the fact in our minds. Christ's indwelling presence is as truly fact as Columbus' existence five centuries ago, and we hold this truth in our minds with the same conviction.

Now we are in a position to state our difficulty in more positive terms. While we are able to **comprehend** Christ (receive the knowledge of His presence), we are not able to **apprehend** Him (lay hold of His person). Comprehend and apprehend are two different things. We can learn of Christ, but we may not reach or apprehend His person — He is Spirit.

All of man's tools and equipment for life on the earth are physical. Even reason and logic must be considered as belonging to the physical realm for they are limited to space and time. Our senses are physical, and we have no equipment for communicating with spirit-beings on the spirit level. There are people who claim to have access to the spirit world, but it is interesting to note that the "spirit" is reported as having produced some physical phenomenon. He has to rap on a table or produce something that can be received by the senses. This is all that man in the finite state has to work with.

There is no way for Christians to know Christ as they know each other; yet His presence is every bit as certain. Were the nation's president to walk into the room where you are now reading, your whole bearing and attitude

173

would suddenly change. You'd feel very self-conscious. You would guard your speech — after you caught your breath. Were he to make his abode in your home, your whole life would be changed and geared to the fact of his presence there with you. We know this would be the case — but think of it, the Son of God has walked through the door of our hearts to take up His abode within us, and we scarcely reflect the staggering fact! To be sure, changes do occur, but they are found only as we become truly aware of the fact of His presence.

We Need Physical Representations of Spiritual Truths

"DO THIS IN REMEMBRANCE OF ME"

God is well aware that man cannot apprehend or lay hold of spiritual beings. Even spiritual truths are often meaningless without some physical representation. The Lord instituted the communion because of this very need in man. When He said, "Do this in remembrance of me,"

and lustful purpose, but they are given
d and creative functions. They should be
ng with the other talents we have from
of this fascinating device, Christians can
piritual presence of Christ. He can take
ally speak within their own minds. The
tion becomes something of a meeting place
pirit world and the physical world and won-
des a great oasis amidst the desert of God-
ions. Our own drives and physical appetites
non-spiritual direction too. The sanctified
s the only haven.

sical organism resists prayer. How unnatural
and read the Bible. Going to church can
bit, yes, but still it is very unnatural. The
will occur only when the discipline of making
ecomes a serious task. We have to impose
e upon ourselves. It will involve the
r lives as well as every device on which we
hands. Books, Christian films, church exer-
altar and a host of other items are needed
earnestly gear ourselves to the fact of His
Habits must be cultivated which will fix the
indwelling in our awareness.

using physical representations to help us
ualize the unseen Lord, we must avoid the
tholic error of substituting a visual aid (statues)
the one we worship. That is, the family altar
but a tool. So is the Bible. So is anything we
to give reality to Christ's presence in our
es. When we allow an aid to worship to
sume a dominant place BETWEEN us and
esus, it becomes an abomination. Even church-
oing can be idolatrous when it takes the place
f intimate fellowship with Jesus.

He gave His disciples a visual aid. Here was something
to which they could literally lay hold. Receiving the death
of Christ, as well as His life, is not an easy concept to
visualize. Yet the simple partaking of a broken wafer
beautifully pictures the first half of the truth. Putting the
cup to the lips and draining its contents crystallizes and
makes real a truth that would otherwise be stored in some
remote corner of the brain. Through active participation
in the communion celebration, the believer "gets his teeth"
into a physical representation of the idea, so to speak. The
human senses come into action and allow the spiritual
work of Christ done for man to take on new and living
significance.

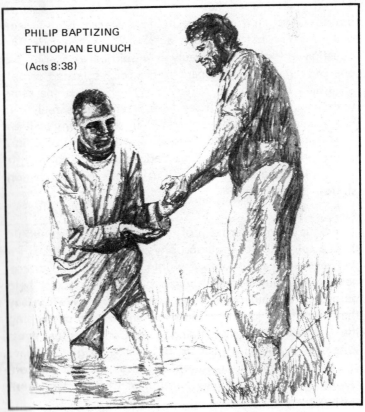

PHILIP BAPTIZING
ETHIOPIAN EUNUCH
(Acts 8:38)

Baptism is another visual aid. Here again, something spiritual that has happened to the believer is expressed in physical terms. The understanding is greatly aided when the emotions and senses can participate in an exercise dramatizing what we, in our heads, know to be true. Through these means a person's whole being can enter into the experience and the reality is driven home with astonishing clearness. God's genius and wisdom is exalted in His giving of the ordinances to the church. By themselves they are meaningless actions, but dramatizing spiritual truth, they become divine vehicles of communication.

This feature applies to other areas of our existence besides Christian truths. Beauty, for instance, is an unseen reality. Who has ever seen a "chunk" of beauty? The question is foolish, for beauty is a spiritual concept. No one can behold beauty apart from a color-splashed sunset, an artist's brush, or an attractive woman. It is the same with love. No one can see love. While it is real, it is not visible to man unless it comes in some form of finite expression. Love has to be found in some kind of action, or its presence remains concealed. There is no way to know that love exists unless it is manifested or demonstrated in deeds.

So it is with the truth of Christ. His presence within us is a spiritual fact requiring physical representations, for we have no way to keep it within our immediate awareness. The truth of Jesus' precious indwelling is not held before us without some effort on our part. We can say that part of our job is to find ways and means of keeping the truth of the Lord's abiding before our spiritual eyes. Whatever it takes, we should be willing to give. There can be no life-changing surrender unless we become constantly impressed and fully mindful of Christ's permanent presence within us.

When we arise in the morning with the sunlight streaming in the window, those beams should instantly remind us that He is the Light of the World. Within the cloistered sanctuary of our imagination we can speak to Him, "Good morning, Lord. I pray my life may shine for you this day even as the sun rays brighten this room." When we slip on our clothes we can say to Him, "I thank you, my Saviour, that I wear Your righteousness." Washing becomes another devotional experience, for as the water of the faucet rinses away the uncleanness, we can tell Him, "Oh, how I praise You, Lord, that Your blood has washed away my guilt of sin." Were someone else to hear us, they'd laugh, but we know that He hears. The fact that we are learning to imagine His presence does not mar the truth a bit. His presence is unquestioned; the Holy Spirit's testimony settles that. We seek only to give His presence a **reality** that will change our lives.

Sitting at the breakfast table signals the need to fill our hearts with His Word — we are feeding more than one man now. The new man is hungry, too, and he longs for a different kind of bread. Driving to work in the car becomes another spiritual delight. If we are alone with Him, then others won't be disturbed if we sing together or even laugh. What a wonderful time to talk of the things that we wish to do together that day, or perhaps there are some dear Christian brothers who have a need that we might discuss.

The time at the shop is actually no different. That work, too, can be done in the presence of Jesus; in fact the boss will be greatly impressed with the obvious joy and delight shown by the Christ-aware Christian. The wife left at home finds the quiet after the morning rush the best time to go over the prayer list with her Lord while doing the dishes. These disciplines make talking to Jesus a part of normal life. That's what it should be. Talking to Jesus is the normal experience for the man living in God's power. This is really practicing the presence of Christ.

Well, its easy to see what such a life routine accomplishes. We are trying to make the "new man" as real as the "old man." We are seeking to be as much aware of the "fact man" as we are of the "feeling man." It is not easy to surrender to a Christ that is unreal. To most Christians, Jesus is seated on a throne somewhere out in the blue of the sky, and His literal existence within them is scarcely known. A distant Christ doesn't matter too much, but the indwelling Son of God does—if His presence **is recognized.** Jesus doesn't bother anyone if He's not recognized. Thus recognition of the indwelling Christ becomes the **secret** of Christian victory — a **secret** whose key words are **"IMAGINATION** and **DISCIPLINE."** How it must hurt Him when multitudes of His very own live as though He did not exist. How different it becomes when they learn to practice His presence.

Often, the one thing that can make a marriage succeed is **experimentation.** Here's a subject that is vital to our union with Christ. It will take constant experimentation if ways are to be found that will make His abiding not only real, but natural as well. Jesus wants to be enjoyed as well as served, for that is an important feature of the next life. When the experience of living with Christ becomes real, natural and fun, then there's no problem as to which man gets our surrender. Anyone **really living** with Jesus would choose no other Master.

Of course, one day it will be over and we will no longer have to gear a physical life to a spiritual person. We will be aware of the spirit world ourselves and can then know Jesus as we know each other now. We will then "know even as we are also known." As longingly as we look toward that day, we are now living a life that requires us to walk with our God by faith; a walk ordered by two opposing natures. Victory is found only as Christ and the new nature become as real as the old. A day filled with decisions to please God is a day of victory for the Christian.

VICTORY THROUGH THE INDWELLING CHRIST

MAIN TEACHING (Review and Remember)

1. The believer's choice between two natures makes his life one of constant struggle.

2. The struggle of the Christian life is calculated to produce growth and strength.

3. The new nature makes victory possible in one's life, but does **not guarantee** it.

4. Surrender to the new nature brings Christ's victory in delivering power.

5. Surrender to the new nature is opposed and made difficult by:
   a. The force and pressure of natural earthly life.
   b. The strange and unnatural character of the new life.
   c. The unseen, unheard, and unfelt qualities of the new nature (Christ).

6. Giving reality to the new man makes our Christian decisions less difficult.

7. The new man can be made more real by the use of imagination and discipline.

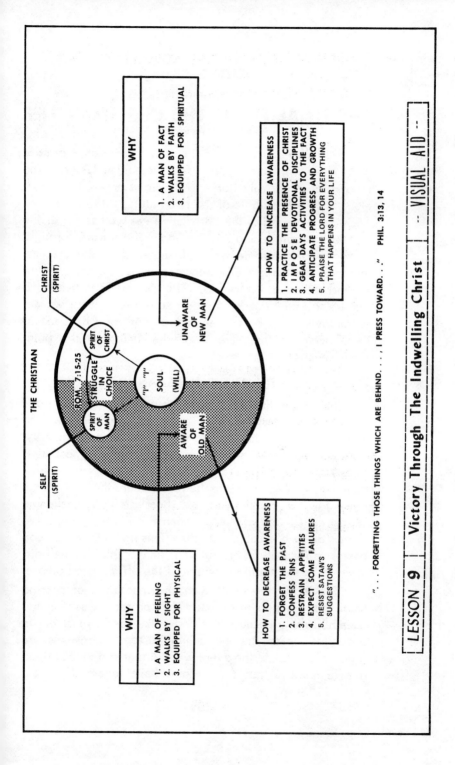

WHY

1. A MAN OF FACT
2. WALKS BY FAITH
3. EQUIPPED FOR SPIRITUAL

HOW TO INCREASE AWARENESS

1. PRACTICE THE PRESENCE OF CHRIST
2. I M P O S E DEVOTIONAL DISCIPLINES
3. GEAR DAYS ACTIVITIES TO THE FACT
4. ANTICIPATE PROGRESS AND GROWTH
5. PRAISE THE LORD FOR EVERYTHING
   THAT HAPPENS IN YOUR LIFE

THE CHRISTIAN

CHRIST
(SPIRIT)

SELF
(SPIRIT)

SPIRIT
OF
CHRIST

SPIRIT
OF
MAN

SOUL
(WILL)

ROM. 7:15-25
STRUGGLE
IN
CHOICE

UNAWARE
OF
NEW MAN

AWARE
OF
OLD MAN

WHY

1. A MAN OF FEELING
2. WALKS BY SIGHT
3. EQUIPPED FOR PHYSICAL

HOW TO DECREASE AWARENESS

1. FORGET THE PAST
2. CONFESS SINS
3. RESTRAIN APPETITES
4. EXPECT SOME FAILURES
5. RESIST SATAN'S
   SUGGESTIONS

". . . FORGETTING THOSE THINGS WHICH ARE BEHIND. . ., I PRESS TOWARD. . ." PHIL. 3:13, 14

LESSON 9 | Victory Through The Indwelling Christ | -- VISUAL AID --

CHAPTER TEN

THE FINALITY OF THE CHRISTIAN LIFE

God's overall program for man has become increasingly clear with our progress from lesson to lesson. The mechanics of our salvation and its provision are behind us along with the struggle of the two natures. We have seen Christ's pioneering of the Christian life as well as the divine system for reproducing sons of God. These truths brought us to the place where we could enter upon the practical lesson of practicing the presence of Jesus in order to bring His indwelling to awareness. The awareness is needed if we are to know victory through surrender. Now we are to discover why it is vital and urgent for Christians to have victory in their lives and what failure at this point really means.

THE OPPORTUNITY OF THE CHRISTIAN LIFE

"Only one life—'twill soon be past, only what's done for Christ will last." Here's a popular phrase known to almost every Christian today, which, for all its popularity, cries a truth that is scarcely noticed. It is almost as if none dares to face the enormity of its significance. Now, however, we have come to the place where this vital theme must grip our minds with its heart-probing challenge. Facing the **finality** of the Christian life is the unavoidable climax of such a course as this. This life, which so soon passes, is not only brief, but very final. This we shall discover to be the startling content of the oft repeated phrase.

Previously we dealt with the mechanics of passing from this life into the next. The process was labeled "death" simply because the body, like seeds, must die in order to release the indwelling person. Christians are urged to anticipate the event without fear and to look upon it as a glorious transition. Some have regarded the experience as simple as closing of one pair of eyes and opening another. This much is true, for one phase of life ceases and the other commences in the same split second. Were it not for the grief which attends the loss of friends, Christians could almost shout with joy when the event approaches. This is only part of the story, however.

Paul makes a strange comment about death, "The last enemy that shall be destroyed is death" (1 Cor. 15:26). Right in the middle of his thrilling resurrection message he describes death as the "last enemy" of the Christian. What a strange name to give to this feature of life that is generally spoken of in very glowing terms. Why should Paul speak this way? What ominous foreboding does he see in death that he should give this name of "enemy?"

Do we not think of death as the time when we shall be with our departed loved ones? Does not death usher in the promised rest and bliss of heaven? Is not this the time when the struggle of the two natures is finally over and we can enjoy the delights of God's riches? Why, some even feel that regardless of any waste in their lives here, heaven will suddenly offer them the fruitful end of the "horn of plenty;" that it doesn't matter what has happened here on earth, the experience of death will make everything somehow all right. If this is so, then death is indeed the **"last friend."** Why does Paul not give this name instead of calling it the "last enemy" of the Christian?

There is a feature of death that indeed makes it the last enemy. It can justly be called that when it is looked upon as the **end of all opportunity** for the growth and investment of the Christian's life. We do have just this one life here on earth to grow and be like Christ; just one chance to obey and serve Him with our talents. **Personal** growth and personal investment come to an end at physical death, and the wasted opportunity of this life becomes a permanent loss.

It is a serious thing to say that any waste of our lives here on earth results in a **permanent** loss that cannot be made up on the other side of death. This is the frightful implication of the phrase, "Just one life . . ."; we do have just one life in which we may grow into the likeness of the Lord and serve Him for the sake of the rewards which He offers. There will be no second chance: no make-up classes or additional opportunities. The door of opportunity closes when we leave these bodies.

"LAY UP FOR YOURSELVES"

HEAVEN

INVEST IN CHRIST NOW—
ENJOY THE
REWARD FOREVER!

EARTH

Believers serving Christ during their time on earth accumulate treasure in heaven. Everything done for Jesus that is performed out of love, adds that much more to the believer's ETERNAL wealth. This treasure is genuine. It will be waiting for the Christian when he gets there. The nice thing about it is that it can be enjoyed FOREVER! Rewards received on earth last for the moment only and cannot be taken with us when we go to heaven.

The only treasure that men will have in heaven is that which they have **earned.** Being in heaven is salvation; that's another issue, we're not discussing that. This has to do with our status after we get to heaven; what we **have** when we get there and what we **are like.** With respect to our rewards, Jesus speaks very plainly, "Lay up **for yourselves** treasure in heaven . . . " (Matt. 6:20). The point of His remark is that unless we do this for ourselves, we will have none. This is not something that God does for us, we do it for ourselves. Clearly this has reference to our **works** for Christ.

The Lord referred to our earthly life as an opportunity for investment. He spoke of it in terms of percent. Those who invest their time, money, talent, and energy in Him, "shall receive a hundredfold," He said (Matt. 19:29). Now one fold is 100%. Therefore a hundred fold is **ten thousand per cent!** That's some interest. Nothing on earth offers that kind of a return for your investment. The big money people are happy to get 6%. Jesus offers us the privilege of investing all of our lives, 24 hours a day, at this fantastic rate. Those who refuse to use their lives for Christ will have NOTHING when they get to heaven.

 Some feel that they can live this life any way they want after coming to Christ; that salvation is good enough by itself. They feel it is not necessary to serve Christ with all of the talents they have received from Him; that if they are saved, somehow God will make everything turn out all right when finally they go to be with Him. They reason, since He is all-powerful, He can make things work to suit Himself, and that He will adjust for all their waste and indifference. What a terrible blindness this is! Nothing could be

further from the truth. God has ordained that this life is the place where man can (1) freely elect to know Him, (2) grow to be like Him, and (3) serve Him. He will not contradict Himself.

The life that is lived here in the flesh is a **single** golden opportunity which forever passes away at physical death. To ignore this fact, and to indifferently throw away this opportunity hoping for God to overlook our half-heartedness, is to possess an ostrich-like "head in the sand" attitude that will bring its terrible consequence at the time of judgment. The life on earth will be found to determine the nature and character of the life in heaven.

THE JUDGMENT OF THE CHRISTIAN LIFE

The Scripture unequivocally asserts there is a judgment for each life at the time of physical death, ". . .it is appointed unto men once to die, but after this, the judgment" (Heb. 9:27). For the Christian this event is called the Judgment Seat of Christ; for the unsaved man, the Great White Throne Judgment. All men are judged, saved and unsaved alike. The judgments that are awarded are based upon past performance and are **eternal**. The past definitely determines the future.

Our interest is in the Christian and his judgment. At the time of death his life development and works suddenly cease and are evaluated to determine his future status. During his lifetime on earth the believer is completely responsible for the development of his own person into the likeness of Christ and the investment of his talents and substance. He has full and exclusive control over these areas. It is really a stewardship. God entrusts him with this bit of sovereignty and expects him to be faithful in that trust. It brings responsibility, however; a responsibility for which the Christian must give account when the time arrives.

 Paul refers to this accounting directly in several places. It is one of his most urgent messages to his readers. These are uncompromising words, "So then every one of us (Christians) must give account of himself to God" (Rom. 14:12). Paul says that the whole of life is to be looked upon as a stewardship which is accounted for as though it really belonged to someone else. Much as a bank endures examination of its books and operational policies when the examiner arrives, the Christian undergoes a similar accounting. The bank officials are responsible for handling people's funds; we are responsible for our persons, time, talents, and substance.

The apostle goes on:
We must all appear before the Judgment Seat of Christ; that every one (Christians) may **receive** the things done in his body (time on earth), according to that he hath done, whether it be **good** or **bad** (2 Cor. 5:10).

Paul makes it clear that we are judged for what we have **done.** If the deeds have been good, we will receive reward, but he doesn't stop with that. If the works have been bad, we will receive for that, too. The Greek word is "Kakon" which properly means evil. The Christian's evil deeds definitely affect his judgment. Too often the Christian life is presented as a "bed of roses." "Come and be saved" is the invitation, "after that, everything will be OK. God forgives your sins and nothing else is really important." "Not so," says Paul, "be not deceived; God is not mocked: for whatsoever a man soweth, that shall he also reap" (Gal. 6:7).

189

All of our thoughts and acts affect our future status and reward. Because of the nature of the coming judgment; because of its eternal consequence, Paul's heart fears for the brethren. "Knowing therefore the terror of the Lord, we persuade men . . . " (2 Cor. 5:11). He would plead with men to invest themselves and take advantage of every moment of life because of the seriousness and finality of the Judgment Seat of Christ.

The evil that we do and the failure to invest and use our lives for Jesus results in tragic loss to the believer. When his stewardship accounting reveals a misspent life " . . . he shall suffer **loss,"** says Paul, in one of his clearest references to the judgment event (1 Cor. 3:13-15). A permanent loss that will be a part of the eternal judgment.

There is no point in God's judging lives at all unless the results of that judgment stand forever.

With every judgment the PAST determines the FUTURE. A man sentenced for his part in a shooting is sent to prison for 30 years. His act in the past settled his future for the next 30 years. So with the Christian. What he does on earth settles his future FOREVER! If he serves the Lord faithfully, the judgment will give him a rich reward to enjoy for eternity. If he lives for himself, squandering his life in earthly pursuits, the judgment guarantees he will have NO reward in heaven. And he will stay that way forever. Poverty in heaven is no better than it is on earth, even though a believer does live with Christ in glory. Paul advises us all to seek a better resurrection. That is what he means.

Peter expresses the same urgency, "Pass the time of your sojourn here in fear . . . " (I Pet. 1:17). The beloved John feels the same way, "Now my little children abide in Him . . . and not be **ashamed** before Him at His coming" (I John 2:28). If it were not possible for a Christian to be ashamed at the appearing of Christ, the apostle would not say such a thing. Not only is it possible, but many of God's own are going to be ashamed and there will be great sadness and "weeping and wailing and gnashing of teeth" as the wasted and misspent lives are examined. The justice of God will not be flaunted and made ridiculous. Where would be the justice of God if the Christian (or anyone else) could live any way he wanted to and not have to give a steward's account of his life, substance and talents? These apostles want believers to be glad for the coming day instead of dreading it. But alas, what a time of tragedy and loss it will be for many. Many will be surprised at their own exposure at the Judgment Seat, yet it is doubted that any will complain—"Will not the Judge of all the earth do right?"

The basis of the judgments is not difficult to fathom: each person will be dealt with for what he **has done** as compared with what he **could have done.** Each will be measured against his own capacity for growth and service—not against someone else. The Parable of the Minas makes this unmistakably clear (Luke 19:11-26). Also each man's person will be measured by how much he has grown and matured as compared with how much he could have grown and matured within the opportunities of his earthly life span. This judgment is fair. When we fail to serve and grow, the fault is squarely our own. We can blame no one but ourselves.

Some reading these lines may feel inclined to protest the fact that we are judged on the basis of past performance; that is, for what we ourselves do, offering that the grace and forgiveness of God take care of our defects and failures. They hold that the work of Christ covers everything and that we stand finally shining and arrayed in His righteousness and glory, the past notwithstanding.

Some distinctions have to be made to avoid confusion at this point. There is a confusion in these protests due to the mixing of **forgiveness** with **effect.** The forgiveness of sins and the effect of sins are not the same thing. God forgives our sins because of Christ's atoning work; that is, He does **not punish** us for them, but the **effect** of them still remains. The judgment of our persons and works is not a punishment. There is no punishment for the Christian. That's what forgiveness means. The guilt of sins is that which brings punishment and that is removed from the Christian. He is **not guilty** of anything. He still may suffer loss, however, for his failures; that is only just. Christ's work for us does not make up for **our failure** to grow and serve. Christ's work cares for the **guilt** of our sins only, and the provision of a righteous nature.

A parent may forgive his child for having his bicycle stolen through failure to lock it while at school. The lad is not punished, but he is still minus his bicycle as a result of the disobedience. He suffers loss, yet at the same time his sin is forgiven. This is God's own Law of the Harvest: we reap what we sow. The law must stand. The same holds true with respect to the Christian. God forgives the sin and brings no punishment, yet His justice demands that the reward be just. The matter of **just** reward works two ways: the unfaithful can never be equally compensated with the faithful; that would not be just. This is the clear message of the Parable of the Talents (Matt. 25:14-30).

Here's what we as Christians must face; we are just as good and faithful as we **want** to be. This is a hard fact, and we must face it. We can grow in this life as much as we want to and we can serve the Lord as much as we want to. There are no restrictions placed on us. The only reason we do not grow and use our talents is because we do not please to do so. This is hard for us to admit but we are just as good and faithful as we care to be. In this sense we hold the key to our future in our own hands.

193

We make our own judgment, so to speak, and when we consider that the judgment determines the future, it is easy to understand Paul's plea to "redeem the time." The Judgment Seat makes this life investment an issue of desperate moment, for the character of the future life is determined by it.

THE TWO-FOLD JUDGMENT OF THE CHRISTIAN

If the coming judgment and the opportunity of this life were not so final, we would simply smile at it and pass on our way. It is the fact that death brings an end to **all** of our personal development and investment that makes the matter so urgent. This life on earth, by means of the judgment, affects our heavenly life with Christ. We use the words "judgments" and "rewards," but they have far greater significance when we think that they represent our eternal relationship to Jesus. They are descriptive words, having to do with both our **persons** and our **works.** Our eternal fellowship with God and the jobs we will hold are determined by the lives we live here on earth.

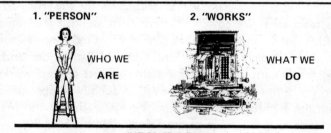

1. "PERSON"	2. "WORKS"
WHO WE ARE	WHAT WE DO

JUDGMENT SEAT

When we stand before God in the judgment, two things will be measured: (1) our persons (how much we've grown like Christ), (2) our works (how much we've done for Him on earth). These two things will determine our nearness to the Lord and the kind of job we'll have in heaven. Those who have worked on their personalities to become like Christ, will be the nearest to Him. Those who invested their lives for Him on earth will have the top jobs in His kingdom. It is foolish not to invest in Christ now, while we have the chance, because we are going to hold those jobs throughout eternity.

The development and judgment of the Christian's person. Physical death brings an end to the development of our persons. In this life we are free to grow into the likeness of Jesus. The divine intention is that we "should be conformed to the image of His Son." This is one of the reasons why we are left on earth after we are saved. God wants us to grow and be like Himself so that we can participate in the future fellowship on the same level with Him.

The possession of the two natures produces the struggle which permits the soul of the believer to grow and be strengthened, and the goal of that growth is the likeness of Christ. God not only designed man to be **with** Him, but to be **like Him.** This likeness is produced by the struggle of physical life on earth. God is long-suffering, but how is the Christian to be long-suffering unless he suffers a long time? God is patient, but how is the Christian to learn patience unless he is in a place of nerve-racking anxiety and disappointment? God is forgiving, but how can the Christian learn to be forgiving unless he is injured? We could go right down the list of divine qualities and find that none of them can be produced without the struggle of this life and the two natures. None of the features listed in Galatians 5:22-23 could ever be found in us without the earthly experience. Only here can we find the things which will produce this fruit in our lives; not in heaven.

Only now can we learn to control our tempers, watch our speech, learn how to act when we've been taken advantage of, serve as peacemakers and be anxious for nothing. In heaven we will be clothed with the new man only, and those things will not be present to exercise the soul. The earth is God's laboratory to polish His sons and to mould them through struggle. Here alone can they learn the lesson that will produce the Christ-like character He so desperately seeks to build in them. The route is suffering first, then glory.

The growing process comes to an end at physical death. The moulding and developing is over and God takes us as we come from the earth "assembly line." The whole program is something like that which takes place in a "photo lab." An exposed film is first put into the developer. There it stays for an appointed time and then it is removed and placed into a solution known as the "fixer." This chemical bath stops the developing process. From then on the negative will always be the same. It will be displayed in wonderful prints after that, however, and show off the skill of the photographer. **The Christian life is like that.**

DEVELOPER   FIXER   DISPLAY

We are in the developer now; this life. **Death is** like the "fixer." We are yanked out of life here and the death-fixing solution brings our developing to an abrupt halt. The product **stays like it is** from that point on, and the Master Craftsman Himself takes it and displays it to the best advantage. It is something like the unveiling of a statue that the sculptor has secretly been producing. On the day of exposure the canvas is whisked away and there it is! It shines as a testimony to his skill. God will take us and display us to our best advantage when the thin "body-canvas" is removed.

People cannot really see us now. They cannot look into our minds to behold the filth and corruption that lurks there. The purity of our motives is not visible to them now, but in the day of revealing (judgment), we will be unveiled and our persons exposed to each other. The growth and development that we have made through earth's opportunity will be manifest. Our hearts and minds and character will show as they really are. The day of death arrests our development and it reveals what has grown.

We enter heaven **just as we are** at the point of death. There's no change in us at all. Death simply unveils us as we are and have grown in the likeness of Christ. If death should come to you, dear reader, you will enter heaven just as you are right now. You will enter heaven the same person. True, the old nature will be gone, but you will be the same soul. Changes in our condition must occur here in this life—they cannot occur in the next. The environment needed for soul growth is not found in heaven. It's a different environment and serves a completely different purpose.

The reason why we cannot grow in the likeness of Christ after death is fairly simple and obvious. No one will be able to trust God and walk by faith in heaven. We'll see Him face to face. Our walk will be by sight then, not faith. We will not be able to suffer any more in order to grow in patience and long-suffering; there won't be any pain or sorrow. We will no longer wait on the promises of God, they will have all been fulfilled. There will be no struggle of the two natures; we will have but one. We will not be able to have victory over sin and temptation; there won't be any around. We cannot triumph

197

over Satan through the power of the Indwelling Christ any longer; that rascal will be finished and gone from us forever. We will not be able to love our enemies; we won't have any. How can we grow in such an environment? We can't. We have just this one life in which to grow like Jesus and every second of it is precious and filled with opportunity that will one day be gone.

An interesting question suggests itself here and the author does not attempt to give a dogmatic answer, but the challenge of it is worthy of our including it. Will we love Jesus any more then, than we do now? Will He be any more precious to us in the next life than He is now? It would seem that we ought to love Him more now and cling to Him very tightly now, for this is the hour of our trial. This is the time of our struggle and tribulation; this is when we need Him so badly. His glory may dazzle us in that day, but His love, mercy and strength are dear to us now. The thought suggests itself that if Jesus is not precious to us now, how can he be precious to us in heaven? If we do not wish to be close to Him here, why should we there? Why should we be **any closer?** We'll leave this for you to decide, dear reader.

In heaven there will be an **unlimited expression** of these persons that have grown on earth. The old nature will be gone, and only the new man will be present. We will be clothed in this righteous new man and can express ourselves through Him. Even though we are granted unlimited expression of our persons in heaven, all that can be expressed is the man that has grown. There can be an infinite revealing of this man—but only as far as he has grown. That was determined by the life on earth. This means that we, with whatever Christ-like maturity we have gained by the time of death, can infinitely express ourselves through the new nature in heaven. Whatever bigness of soul we have will have already been determined on earth. That bigness will be our ability to give ourselves to God. We are designed in the Image of the Giver

Himself, but we **learn to give** on earth, not in heaven. It's easy to see, then, why our earthly probation conditions the life of fellowship to come.

The development and judgment of the Christian's work. Physical death brings an end to our opportunity to freely serve Christ by faith. Our future job in heaven is determined by our faithfulness with what we have here. Once "D" Day arrives, our works will be evaluated at the Judgment Seat, and our new work in heaven permanently established. How Jesus' words do crystallize this truth, " . . . because thou hast been faithful in a very little, have thou authority over ten cities" (Luke 19:17). The future was determined by the past. This is the full meaning of the judgment of God.

There is no limit placed on us now as to how much we can serve the Lord. We can do it sixty minutes out of the hour if we want to. We have unlimited opportunity now in qualifying for our future work (reward). There are no restrictions; everyone has the same opportunity. We have just the one lifetime in which to do it, though, and then comes the old enemy, death. Once we are placed in that "fixer," our jobs are determined along with our persons.

The job we do in heaven will be infinitely performed. It will be suited to us perfectly, for it is based on what we have proved ourselves capable of handling in earth's "qualifying course." This does not mean that it will be monotonous or dull. It will be exciting and infinitely carried out to perfection. There will be nothing static about heaven at all. Both our person and our work will have infinite expression, and we will be set off in the new environment in such a way as to make our contribution to the future fellowship sparkle and bring great joy and gladness to the brethren. We will rejoice in each other in that day and be glad for all that God has done in us and through us. The time of judgment itself will no doubt cause us pangs of remorse when we think back on what we could have been, but as the years of eternity begin to roll, our hearts will thrill to the place and work we have next to Christ. There's no limitation on us here and this is a finite world; surely there'll be no limitation there in the spirit world. Just think how long it will take us to learn to be omnipresent!

Now we can see why it is so important to walk with Jesus moment by moment; why we need to learn how to draw close to Him; to want to be near Him. That's what we'll be doing in the next life. He is the very center of heaven and we are now preparing for that eternal state. We need to begin now learning how to live with Him, for that is all we will do in the next life. We can't shut Him out then as we can now. Serving Him is the same. We need to learn to love serving Him now, for that is all that we will be doing there. If we don't like serving Him, it will have a very definite effect upon the future job.

It would be far better that we get so used to being with Him and serving Him that when death comes, it is not an enemy; it is a friend, for it brings us face to face with Him. Oh, if only we could be so close to Him that the death experience would be simply a matter of saying "Hi . . . Lord." If only we could be so full of Christ and so used to His directions that the transfer from this life to the next wouldn't be noticed by us. Then we could take it in our stride and scarcely be ruffled by it.

Think of Him now. His eyes are on us every second pleading with us to redeem the time and make use of every minute of earth's golden opportunity. He knows this is all we have, and He begs us to consider that our whole future is at stake. "Live unto Me," He says, "and you'll never be sorry. If you could only learn to delight yourself in Me, I am able to give you all the desires of your heart." Dear friend, reading these words, the world and all it offers is not worth having when compared with our Lord's, "Well done." Riches, power and position are tempting and even thrilling, but nothing will be comparable to the one who stands before the majesty of the Great King and hears those words come from His lips. In that day, the kings of the earth would trade all they had and enjoyed just to be in the shoes of a simple, humble servant of Christ. The phrase ought to ring with new meaning now,

> Only one life —
> 'Twill soon be past,
> Only what's done
> For Christ will last.

And why? — "For great is your reward in heaven."

The Lord had much to say about the forthcoming judgment of the believer. It is vital that every Christian know exactly how Jesus means to measure us in that judgment. Those who have this understanding are in a position to make the best possible investment of their lives. Those who don't will surely be sorry. This chapter has barely touched on the matter. If you want to prepare yourself for that awesome moment, you must read my book, **Why Die As You Are!** It provides an in depth picture of the judgment of our person and our works, and shows HOW to get ready for it.

THE FINALITY OF THE CHRISTIAN LIFE

MAIN TEACHING (Review and Remember)

1. Death is popularly taught as the Christian's blissful entrance into heaven, but that is only part of the story.

2. Death brings a judgment to every person whether saved or not.

3. This judgment appraises the life lived on earth and permanently decides one's future status on the basis of past performance.

4. Earthly life is viewed as a stewardship. Christians must account for that stewardship with respect to their **persons** and **works**. God will not overlook wasted lives.

5. God's justice demands some distinctions be made between faithful and unfaithful Christians. The differences between them will be eternal. This does not contradict His mercy which deals with sin's **guilt** only.

6. Death is seen as the "last enemy" of the Christian for it ends his **sole** opportunity for growth and investment in Christ. No waste of the life can be made up later and neither is it automatically cared for by grace.

7. Physical life (faith walk) affords the single privilege for the soul of man to mature in the likeness of Christ. Neither job-determining nor growth producing conditions exist in heaven.

8. Heaven will provide for infinite expression of the **person** as he has developed on earth, and will allow him to perform his pre-determined **task** in the new area of spirit world. Omnipresence, omniscience, and omnipotence will characterize the next type of development. **Soul**-growth is over at death.

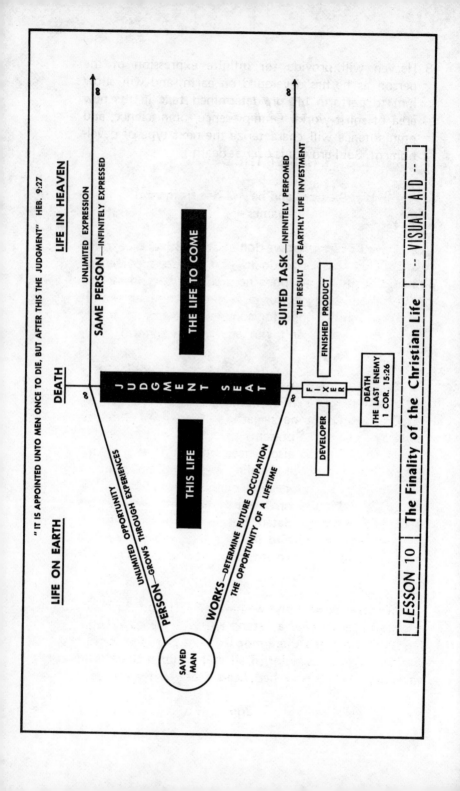

"IT IS APPOINTED UNTO MEN ONCE TO DIE, BUT AFTER THIS THE JUDGMENT" HEB. 9:27

LIFE ON EARTH | DEATH | LIFE IN HEAVEN

UNLIMITED EXPRESSION
SAME PERSON—INFINITELY EXPRESSED

THE LIFE TO COME

JUDGMENT SEAT

SUITED TASK—INFINITELY PERFOMED
THE RESULT OF EARTHLY LIFE INVESTMENT

DEVELOPER   FIXER   FINISHED PRODUCT

DEATH
THE LAST ENEMY
1 COR. 15:26

THIS LIFE

PERSON—GROWS THROUGH EXPERIENCES
UNLIMITED OPPORTUNITY

WORKS—DETERMINE FUTURE OCCUPATION
THE OPPORTUNITY OF A LIFETIME

SAVED MAN

LESSON 10 | The Finality of the Christian Life | -- VISUAL AID --

SOME QUESTIONS?

❶ SHOULD WE RESIST THE DEVIL?

"Resist the devil and he will flee from you!"
—James 4:7

It would seem that we don't have much choice in the matter. God tells us to do it. And He has provided all the authority and weapons needed. Until we learn how to use those weapons for a face to face stand against Satan, we cannot hope for complete and lasting victory in our lives. You can't win any war by ignoring your enemy.

In order that Christians might learn to draw close to Christ and concentrate on building the new man, I have purposely avoided the negative side of our Christian warfare. This book presents the positive approach to victory, but there is also a negative one. That approach is set forth in my book, **Dealing With The Devil.** It offers a four-step plan for dealing directly with Satan. It is patterned after the Lord's experience with Satan in the wilderness. Because Satan has been so successful in blinding God's people to his existence and the way he works to hinder our growth in Christ, I urge you to get a copy.

The apostle Paul says we have a FIGHT on our hands and warns us to take a "stand against" the devil (Eph. 6:11). He even lists the armor God has provided for our warfare. What's the point of all that armor if there is no adversary? Peter, who had been deceived by the devil many times, tells us we must RESIST him (1 Pet. 5:9). But it is the apostle James who guarantees a successful outcome if we will learn how to deal with Satan, "Resist the devil and he will FLEE from you!" That's a promise of God.

Many who love God's Word ignore His warning against Satan. That's like telling Paul Revere to "forget it!" There simply can be no real victory in the Christian life without a FIGHT. The word "victory," means to triumph in battle. The believer who does not learn how to deal with the devil will not go very far on the road to maturity.

Once you know how to order Satan away in the power of the Holy Spirit, using God's Word as a "sword," you will have TWO WEAPONS for victory rather than one. You will be equipped with both positive and negative approaches for winning the battle against the flesh.

You won't be sorry. I promise your life will change. And you'll be thanking God for the terrific help HE has sent into your life.

➋ SUPPOSE WE YIELD TO THE OLD NATURE AND SIN—THEN WHAT?

It's bound to happen. Christians do sin. There are times when we all yield to the old nature and that has to produce sin. It's inevitable. However, since we have our new natures and have received Christ's death for ALL of our sin, sin cannot send us to hell. We must, though, do something about it. The apostle John tells us what that is: "If we confess our sins, He is faithful and just to forgive us our sins and to cleanse us from ALL unrighteousness" (1st John 1:9).

What do we do? We CONFESS our sins. That's our part. Then what does God do? He FORGIVES us. That's His part.

But Satan is not about to let it pass that easily. He moves fast with his accusations when we sin. Terrible thoughts enter our minds. "Now you've done it," he says. "God is really unhappy with you. You can't be as close to Him from now on. You've damaged the relationship with your sin." His penetrating suggestions go on from there. He can get a Christian pretty discouraged—if he listens to that stuff. Yet, his moves are obvious, even if they are subtle.

First, he does his best to keep us from going to God with our sin. He makes us feel so dirty, we don't even want to appear in God's presence. He seeks to ruin our relationship with the Lord. And he can too, if we don't apologize to God for hurting Him with our sin. Then, if he can't keep us from asking God to forgive us, he does his best to hinder our ACCEPTING God's forgiveness. That's one of his neatest tricks.

God is FAITHFUL to forgive our sins when we confess them. The Bible is definite about that. But Christians can have a difficult time **accepting** God's forgiveness. So what do they do then? They simply keep on asking God to forgive them, over and over again. When they ought to be thanking Him for His mercy, they are still begging for forgiveness. Now that is Satan's doing.

The devil knows we must ACCEPT God's forgiveness to enjoy release and maintain fellowship between us and God. He is able to stir such miserable feelings inside us, we think we are NOT forgiven—because we don't FEEL like it. The plain truth is, WE ARE. We must take

God at His Word. When He says we are forgiven, we can depend on it—we are. Those feelings Satan stirs within us don't matter one whit. We must brush them off, thank God for His forgiveness, and go on from there.

Once fellowship is restored, the devil still isn't through. He works constantly to remind us of past failures. If he can get us to think we're useless to God, perhaps we won't bother to press for further victories. Therefore, we have another step to take, even after we have accepted God's forgiveness for our sins. We find that step in Paul's example, ". . .one thing I do: forgetting what lies behind and reaching forward to what lies ahead, I press toward the goal for the prize of the upward call of God in Christ Jesus" (Phil. 3:13-14).

Once God forgives you, says Paul—FORGET IT. Press on! Expect to make mistakes in the Christian walk. They are part of growing up. Most of us get our best learning through mistakes. Yet, it is not our mistakes that are important, but our victories. Who cares how many times a toddler falls down while learning to walk? It's those good steps that really count. So it is with us in our life between two natures. We will sin plenty of times. But we will also move ahead in Christ.

So here it is again: we must confess our sins and accept God's forgiveness to protect our fellowship with Him. But once those sins are forgiven, we are to forget them and get on with the business of living for Him— right now.

3 HOW DO WE GET RID OF THE OLD NATURE?

We don't have to. God doesn't want us to get rid of it. It will be gone soon enough.

When we receive Christ, the Holy Spirit performs spiritual surgery on our souls. The old nature is CUT OFF. This is called circumcision. It is a spiritual circumcision. The fleshly circumcision of the Old Testament pictured this **true** circumcision of the **heart**. In the instant that the old is circumcised away from the soul, the **new** nature is grafted on.

Does this mean that we are rid of the old nature? Far from it. It continues with us, residing in the flesh until the body dies. It is gone the moment the flesh drops off. But in the meantime, the Lord is pleased to have us dwell with two natures. In His wisdom He does not discard the old nature. He USES it to produce the struggle that leads to maturity. We need this struggle. We can't come to manhood in Christ without it. Finally when the Lord has squeezed all He can out of our two-nature struggle, death occurs and we are free of that old nature once-and-for all. We enter heaven with the new nature only.

❹ CAN WE REALLY LIVE THE SPIRIT-FILLED LIFE?

To be Spirit-filled, is to be obsessed with the Spirit's presence and power in one's life. How does a person get that way? He tastes the power of God. He puts himself in a position where God can use Him in power and get a healthy sample of what it is like to move in might. Once he has a real good taste, he gets "TURNED ON," as our young Christians say. And he wants more, a lot more.

Here comes your boy to the breakfast table. Man, does he look different this morning! His hair is neatly combed and his shoes are shined. Not only are his clothes pressed, he's even cleaned his finger nails. What's come over him? You know. There's

209

a new girl friend at school. A new affection has seized his life. I'm sure you are well aware of the transforming power of a new affection.

Communists and those who get excited about various causes get so caught up in what they are doing they will go without food to save more money to further their ideas. I had a friend who built a ham radio station in his garage. He got so excited about speaking to people in foreign lands he would stay up all night to reach some new place. It got to be all he could think or talk about. He was obsessed.

To become obsessed we have to be captured by an idea. The idea that should possess the Christian is obeying the Lord. That means surrender. We have already seen how surrender to either nature allows the devil or the Lord to work through us. Paul says, "To whom we yield ourselves servants to obey, his servants we are." When we yield to the old nature, we act like the devil and he empowers us for the works of the flesh. When we yield to the Holy Spirit, He empowers us for the works of God.

If he really wants to, the Christian can make a real surrender to the Lord. The greater his surrender, the more the Lord can do through him. For example, the Lord asks us to be His witnesses (Acts 1:8). If a believer will make a serious commitment to that command, he can taste the power of God right away. The moment he starts to move, he finds the Holy Spirit moves too. As he gets bolder and attempts more difficult types of witnessing, there is more power.

Then it hits him. God's power is directly proportional to his surrender or obedience. Now that is exciting. In time he finds himself doing things he never believed possible. He also senses he is doing it WITH Christ. When a person is able to MOVE in the Spirit's might **as though it were his own,** he gets drunk with joy. He is soon HOOKED on it. It becomes an obsession. Everywhere he goes, he wants to exalt Jesus—that the power of God might flow through him! In time his whole life is caught up in it and he is every bit as obsessed as the lad with a new girl friend or a civil rights champion.

Surrender is the key. The more we surrender to the Holy Spirit, the more He is able to do with us. The more He does with us, the more excited we get. The greater our excitement, the higher our obsession.

There are **degrees** of surrender. Simply moving the arrow to the new nature side, does NOT bring the full power of God's Spirit into one's life. That arrow can be thick, or it can be thin. Just as a tiny strand cannot carry as much electricity as a heavy cable, neither can half-hearted surrender produce as much power in one's life as all out obedience.

The obsessed Christian is a dedicated man. His whole life is wrapped up in Jesus. Serving Christ is all he can think about, it is all he cares about. He eats and sleeps Christ. His life is completely regulated by God's Word and impelled by God's Spirit. He is a "one-thing" Christian. This one thing I do, he says, I forget what is behind me and I press on to the prize of the high call in Christ. He has his eye on the judgment seat. He is excited about his job in heaven. More than anything else he wants to hear that, "Well done, thou good and faithful servant."

Yes, we can live a Spirit-filled life. All we have to do is sample what it means to obey Jesus and taste His power. Once we do, we'll want more. When we become obsessed, we are filled.

recommend witnessing. It's the quickest way to sample God's power. You get a real taste the first time you try it—**if you go at it right**.

The only way to tackle any serious program is to start at the bottom and move up gradually. Why? If you get off to a bad start, it can make you sour on the whole thing. Satan would like that. Because the first steps of witnessing are so critical, the Lord has given us a systematic method for teaching witnessing that allows you to sample the Spirit's power with your very first attempt. You can imagine what that does for you.

This approach is called the Ladder-Method. You know how a ladder works. It takes you to a good height— one step at a time. As a man cannot go from the ground to the roof of his house without a ladder, neither can a Christian go from silence to active witnessing without a PLAN for breaking the distance into easy steps.

See the ladder on page 215? Those 10 steps lift you from silence to action. As you advance up the ladder, you acquire more and more skill. There is a slight increase in threat with each advance, but you don't mind. Your previous action with the Holy Spirit strengthens you. You are ready for it. Before long you display a sweet poise as you move among people witnessing in the power of the Spirit.

• Now there are two ways to learn this method:

(1) You can refer to the list of books in the back and order a copy of **Witnessing Made Easy**. It explains the techniques for all the actions. (2) Or, you can take the

course from PC with me as your personal coach. All ten lessons have been prepared as a correspondence course.

● You do NOT receive all ten lessons at once. You start off with two. That way you can be working on one while the other is in the mail. You carry out specific action-assignments. This is not a pencil/paper program. You make action reports for each rung of the ladder. As soon as I receive one report, the next lesson is mailed to you.

There are three things to do to enroll in the course:

1. Find the application form, p. 217. Read it and fill it out. Sign it. From the information on this application a permanent record is made for you here at PC headquarters and a chart is used to plot your progress.

2. Sit down and write a letter to me telling how you KNOW you are saved. I want you to put your salvation experience on paper. To do so, ask yourself . . . **"What right do I have to call myself a born-again Christian?"** Think too about the ways you reassure yourself you are safe in the Lord. Put it all on paper, describing the best you can the mechanics of your surety in Christ. It doesn't have to be long, just factual. I am not interested in your spelling or handwriting.

Don't try to satisfy me with your statement, satisfy yourself.

This action is not as simple as it sounds. To put things of this nature on paper, a person must first process them in his mind. It often takes a lot of mental energy to reshape scattered and unfocused ideas into a solid statement, but that's what I want. If your experience in Christ is vague and shadowy, this can be a rewarding assignment. The witness-life requires a firm base. It is the launching pad from which you will go into orbit, so it must be solid.

3. Along with your application and salvation letter, enclose the enrollment fee—$10.00. You will understand this is not a money making venture when I tell you the cost of the materials for this course runs $8.38. Handling and lesson grading is not a part of that total. The purpose of this course is solely to activate saints for Christ, with the confidence that our "profit" will be laid up and waiting for the day when we will see you there!

Here are the advantages of climbing the witnessing ladder this way:

- Your work is more determined and systematic with the discipline of accounting to someone else, as reinforced by the heart-treasure principle when you invest the $10.00.

213

- If you are a pastor or teacher, you can systematically bring your people along a step or two behind you. You can put the know-how to work in your group even as you ascend the 10 rungs of the ladder.

- Each time we receive an action report, you receive a prayer-boost by name as your report goes before the Friday night prayer-band.

- If you begin to show excessive lag in your reporting, a follow-up letter will spur you on to increased dedication.

- You receive a membership card and **permanent number** when you reach the fifth rung of the ladder. This number can be used to earn an **immediate discount** on all supplies you order from PC. In time this can return the cost of the course.

- Upon completion of the course, you receive the silver PC pin. These coveted pins are kept locked in a safe, and there is no way to secure one except by completing all ten action steps of the witnessing ladder. They truly certify the wearer to be an active and skilled witness for Christ.

- You can take your time. Some take as long as one year to complete the course. The fastest is three months. You advance to the next higher rung after you have learned to be **comfortable** witnessing at the lower level. The pressure is your own ambition to go as far as you can in Christ.

Go to the place where you do your letter writing. Take pen and paper and get your salvation experience down in black and white. You'll enjoy sweet exhilaration doing just that much. The thrill of getting started on a new career for Christ brings the first excitement. Satan will urge you to put it off. Don't listen to him. The Holy Spirit is ready to work with you now! As soon as you get that letter on its way to me, you will have taken the first step toward. . .

A SPIRIT-FILLED LIFE!

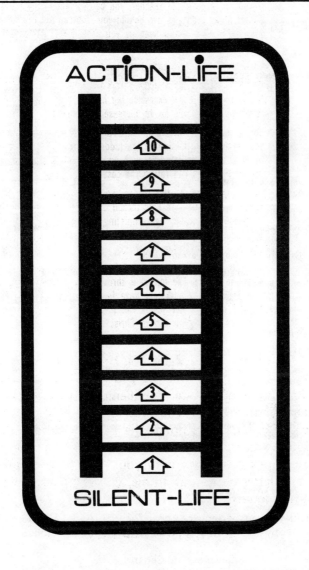

ACTION-LIFE

10
9
8
7
6
5
4
3
2
1

SILENT-LIFE

Becoming a witness is easier — one step at a time.

SAMPLE LETTER Date................................

Dear "C.S."

I have been reading "Witnessing Made Easy" and I want to be a witness for our Lord Jesus. I know that I am saved because. . .

INSTRUCTIONS

Complete your letter in a paragraph or two and don't worry about:

1. Spelling

2. Handwriting, though I do have to read it. Use a typewriter if you want to.

3. Grammar or sentence arrangement.

4. Lack of education. If you can read this book, you have enough education to be a vigorous witness.

5. What I think of your letter. I will be looking only at your experience, not you.

HINTS:

1. Do you have a favorite text on which you rest your salvation?

2. Is there a date or event you can recall when you opened your heart to Jesus.

3. Are there ways in which you re-establish your heart in Christ when doubts cross your mind?

4. Think of the actual transaction that takes place when someone receives the gift of eternal life.

I am glad we can become personal friends. And I will look forward to receiving the free witnessing helps you mentioned.

Sincerely in Christ,

Signed..

216

witnessing course BY MAIL
application

PERSONAL CHRISTIANITY
Box 549
Baldwin Park, Calif. 91706 (213) 338-7333

Date_____

Full Name _____

Complete Address _____

City, State, Zip _____

Minister __ Teacher __ Layman __ Housewife __ Student __

Name, Address local church _____

Your occupation _____

Do you receive a copy of PERSONAL CHRISTIANITY
regularly? _____

I want to be a witness for our Lord Jesus. I hereby apply
for the action-course you offer. Enclosed is $10.00 to
cover the cost of the lessons and materials needed for the
assignments.

Check one below:

My salvation experience letter is enclosed _____

You already have my salvation letter _____

As the Lord strengthens my witness-life, I grant PERSONAL
CHRISTIANITY permission to use my testimony for the
purpose of strengthening other Christians.

Signed _____

217

No. 235 ■ TEACH DYNAMIC TRUTHS
by C. S. Lovett
$2.95 ■ (3 for $7.50)

This teacher's guide is companion to the book you have in your hands. It shows how to present the ten dynamic truths at the personal level or at a class level. One does NOT have to be an experienced teacher to use this approach for coaching another person in the Spirit-filled life. The techniques are simple and the lessons are taught in the informal atmosphere of one's home (if used at the personal level.) Sunday school teachers will also appreciate the added insights found in this book.

(paperback, illustrated, teacher's outlines and visuals for each of the ten lessons)

OTHER TITLES by C. S. LOVETT
MENTIONED IN THIS BOOK

No. 510-DEALING WITH THE DEVIL Student's
Text $3.95
No. 520-WHY DIE AS YOU ARE! $1.95
No. 101-WITNESSING MADE EASY Student's
Text $2.95
No. 502-DEATH MADE EASY $1.00

THE ABOVE ITEMS AND FREE CATALOG OF
ALL DR. LOVETT'S WORKS ARE AVAILABLE
FROM

PERSONAL CHRISTIANITY
BOX 549,
BALDWIN PARK,
CALIFORNIA 91706
(213) 338-7333

SINCE 1951

Brother Lovett was saved through his "accidental" attendance at a minister's conference where he eavesdropped the conversation of a group of nationally known Christian leaders. There he overheard a discussion on the mechanics of salvation. For years he had been under conviction, yet no one troubled to introduce him to Christ. Armed with the necessary insight for the salvation experience, he hurried home to share it with his wife, Marjorie.

Together they knelt and invited Christ to come into their hearts. This delayed salvation experience accounts for his burden to do away with the vague and shadowy notions of Christianity and present the truths of God's Word man to man. He hates religious double-talk. His decision to trust Christ also resulted in the loss of his sizeable personal fortune as well.

A graduate of California Baptist Theological Seminary, he holds the M.A. and B.D. degrees conferred Magna Cum Laude. He has completed graduate work in Psychology at Los Angeles State College and holds an honorary doctorate from the Protestant Episcopal University in London. He is a retired Air Force Chaplain with the rank of Lt. Colonel.

DR. LOVETT is pastor of PC

Pastor Lovett is the author of the books and tools produced by Personal Christianity. Able to express the profound things of God in simple, practical language, his writings strengthen Christians the world over. The advent of his "Soul-Winning Made Easy," has drastically changed evangelism methods in America, while the anti-satan skill offered in his "Dealing with the Devil," has alerted multitudes to their authority over our enemy through Christ.

PERSONAL CHRISTIANITY IS ..

A local church with a literature ministry.

We are incorporated under the Laws of the State of California as a local church.

We not only provide a worship center for the residents of the area, but exist as a "ministry of helps" [1 Cor 12:28] toward the "Body of Christ."

PC is not affiliated with any denomination, organization or council of churches.

God has given PC the task of producing the spiritual mechanics for personal obedience to the Great Commission and maturity in the Christian life. Unique, know-how tools are developed within the church and made available to God's people everywhere. Our outreach is by means of the U.S. Postal system which makes possible *personal contact* with individuals and churches across the land and throughout the world.

We bear the name PERSONAL CHRISTIANITY because we seek to involve people personally with the Lord Jesus, the Holy Spirit and the Great Commission.

All who care about Christ are welcome to worship with us. Those further interested in "equipping Christians for action," are invited to invest their talents and strengths with ours. We are interested in every Christian and church willing to take a vigorous stand for Christ in these gloomy days.

221